Letters from the American Desert

Also by Frederick Glaysher

The Parliament of Poets: An Epic Poem

The Bower of Nil: A Narrative Poem

Into the Ruins: Poems

The Myth of the Enlightenment: Essays

The Grove of the Eumenides: Essays on Literature, Criticism, and Culture

Crow Hunting: Songs of Innocence

Edited

Robert Hayden, *Collected Prose; Collected Poems*

Letters *from the* American Desert

Signposts of a Journey
A Vision

Frederick Glaysher

Earthrise Press

www.fglaysher.com

Library of Congress Cataloging in Publication Data

Glaysher, Frederick, 1954-
Letters from the American Desert: Signposts of a Journey, A Vision / Frederick Glaysher.
xi, 171 pages ; 23 cm
1. Glaysher, Frederick—Biography. 2. Poets, American
3. Religion, Baha'i
I. Title

PS3557.L37 Z48 2008 816/.54 2008922794

Hardcover ISBN-13: 978-0-9670421-1-4
ISBN-10: 0-9670421-1-9

Earthrise Press®
P. O. Box 81842, Rochester
Michigan 48308-1842 USA
www.EarthrisePress.Net

In memory of Robert and Elinor Gaines

Contents

Preface

"A man travels the world over in search of what he needs and returns home to find it." —George Moore

Proverbial wisdom and intuitions can be more sustaining than all the cerebral abstractions of a century. Where one's first memories are formed can become a touchstone of reality, a yardstick with which to measure irreality. The suburbs can seem to float between the two, like the soul between two worlds, living out its allotted time. The challenge is what we make of it.

Rochester, Michigan, my hometown—a little bourgeois bedroom community of engineers and other commuters, running the automotive engine of the world, stalled of late, business and *bürgermeisters*, no nonsense, and the charm of rolling hills and oak trees, country farms out the school bus window, the nineteenth century red-brick storefronts of Main Street Americana, foundations that were built to last.

Nostalgia aside, life's journey took me elsewhere, eagerly escaping, with the enthusiasm of youth, the intellectually stifling atmosphere of materialism, but not before a time of solitary study, just a little north in Oakland Township, living on an old farm on Paint Creek, walking through the woods of the gentle valley, trying on the mantle of Robert Frost and other poets, striking out on my own to find out who I was as a writer, as a soul, taking refuge in Emerson's advice of self-reliance. My friends went off to universities, the usual road, while I chose the freedom of independent study, loving to read, relishing the imagination and all its joys, sensing that for me if I went to a university too early I would end up thinking just like everybody else. Better to follow the example of real poets, like Frost and Walt Whitman, and "loafe and invite my Soul." Search myself for the truth. Confront life and the masters directly. Pray to God to guide me. Eventually, I felt I had studied long enough alone, and was ready for formal study, other people, could hold my own against the stultifying atmosphere of college drudgery, made my way elsewhere and to the University of Michigan. The soul's journey can be a long journey, but if we listen carefully, she will lead us aright, through all vicissitudes and trials, guide us through prayer, as by the hand. Little did I know she would lead me back here one day.

The letters are to Mrs. Elinor Gaines, whom I met during a brief return to my hometown in 1978, a few years after becoming a Bahai. I met her and her husband Robert Gaines through the Bahai community of Rochester, attending a Bahai meeting at their home in Christian Hills. In 1987, he was among the 153 people killed in the accident of Northwest Airlines Flight 255 at Detroit Metropolitan Airport, on take-off, crashing in the middle of Interstate 94, a devastating loss for Elinor.

Later, living in Illinois and Arizona, I thought of the letters of John Keats to an older acquaintance, when I began occasionally to write Elinor, already in her 70s. My letters became a way for me to reflect on my work and study, on the fears and worries of the time in global transformation. Like many observers, I could not imagine the Cold War could result in anything other than Armageddon. Humbling to think of that now. Perhaps I appear to have been wrong about Gorbachev and Perestroika. Perhaps we've moved on to other fears, though the dread specter looms about the same.

My grappling for a new form seeks to understand all of that, how to grow beyond the limits of contemporary consciousness, the shorthand of Romanticism, Modernism, and Postmodernism. Academic clichés. The soul hears a different music, a higher song supernal. It is one of love, that seemingly fragile word, what Baha'u'llah called, talking of every age and dispensation, "the law of Love which, like unto a fountain, flows always and is never overtaken by change."

The spelling of Bahai varies during its time in the West and its passage through Bahai denominations. There can be distinctions of meaning. The apostrophe and diacritics were added after 1921. I've come to prefer the Anglicized form, in common usage since as early as 1900.

Frederick Glaysher

Oakland Township, Michigan

January 23, 2008

To be a Bahai simply means to love all the world;
to love humanity and try to serve it;
to work for universal peace
and universal brotherhood.

—Abdul-Baha

Letters from the American Desert

1988 - 1994

Searle Drive
Normal, Illinois

3 November 1988

Dear Elinor,

Last year I was very saddened to read in *The American Baha'i* of Bob's death. At the time I had of course no idea of the circumstances but felt quite grieved, remembering what a good man he was and his personal kindness to me. I sincerely prayed for his well-being and hope he has somehow found solace beyond what we can understand. Please accept my inadequate and overdue condolences.

During the last year I've attended several functions sponsored by the local chapter of the United Nations Association. Adlai Stevenson was from the twin city area here. I must say it's rather dispiriting to observe the loss of commitment to the UN Charter and the decline of the institution itself, so strikingly similar to the collapse of the League of Nations. Brian Urquhart so rightly points out in his 1987 autobiography that the USSR has never had the slightest interest in developing a world organization. What other hope do we have but that? As the Guardian assures us, man will eventually learn from the bitter experience of this century.

With sincere best wishes,

Fred Glaysher

Searle Drive
Normal, Illinois

27 February 1989

Dear Elinor,

I'm sorry not to have written you earlier. Just before I wrote you last I had packed my manual typewriter away and vowed I would never take it out again, so tired had I become of its dust-infected keys. Then about the end of the year I finally acquired a computer, but had to spend a few months learning how to use it and getting caught up on several manuscripts that have been languishing too long.

My sister made it quite clear to me that her friendship with you means a great deal to her. I'm grateful that you both have someone who can feel and understand your grief somewhat. I'm sorry. Words really are so inadequate.

Yes, the emphasis has become almost totally on the administrative order and teaching. Pity.

I did find Bob's journal interesting, though he and you both give me more credit than I deserve. I regret I didn't know him better, but back then I was so involved with my own intense struggles and still so immature, so half-formed, and poorly read. Often I don't feel I've made much headway, though comparatively I know there's much to be thankful for. I hope I don't shock you, but I don't believe I'm one of the spiritual souls. During the last several years I've drunk too deeply at the fount of nihilism for that to be the case. I feel too poignantly the truth of the observation of the Russian writer Aleksandr Solzhenitsyn: "The entire twentieth century is being sucked into the vortex of atheism and self-destruction." That to me is the bitter truth of the state of the soul today. I'd say the Guardian came increasingly to realize it too, as in that last terrifying Ridvan message of his in which he speaks of the "retributive calamity which . . . must, sooner or later, afflict a society which, for the most part, and for over a century, has turned a deaf ear to the Voice of God's Messenger in this day." Ominous words are those, made more so by forty-odd years of waning commitment to the UN Charter and the ever more precipitous descent into the vortex.

I found the excerpt you chose for Bob's tombstone quite moving and beautiful. I was struck by them and by your comment on old cemeteries. For the first time in years I recalled noticing prior to becoming a Baha'i how rare verses of any religious sentiment were in cemeteries after 1840 or so.

With sincere wishes for your abiding solace and peace of mind,

Fred Glaysher

Searle Drive
Normal, Illinois

1 September 1989

Dear Eleanor,

We're glad we were able to meet last weekend. I'm sorry, though, that we didn't have enough time and composure to discuss anything properly. I'm afraid what with the children and the necessary proprieties of reestablishing a relationship, much was left unsaid. On the other hand I worry that too much was said without adequate explanation. Ah life! We human beings never seem to get it right! Well, I hope you'll understand or be forbearing.

The administrative order has come a long way but still has so very far to go. Louhelen Bahai School and the rest are something to be thankful for yet really lag so far behind what they should be. I'm one of those souls the Guardian mentions somewhere when he states that not everyone should be expected to be interested and involved in the administrative order—or even capable of being involved—I know I lack the necessary managerial ability and temperament though I appreciate the fundamental importance of the administration. I used to worry about this or try to be something other than what I am. Robert Hayden had a very clear understanding of the dilemma. On one occasion he told me, "How would I have ever written a thing had I been involved in all of that?" This can be difficult or impossible for others who are gun-ho on building it all up today, right now—but surely a firm foundation requires many types of self-sacrifice, none of them easy.

After leaving your house we were quite concerned when we realized that some of your comments may have intimated a desire to give up, shall I say, on life. You know better than anyone else what is right for you, in the grief of your own heart, but I feel one must never give up, let go, however it should be put. You could perhaps live another ten or more years, if the willingness to accept the living sacrifice of a new life, dedicated to, well, whatever in your inmost soul you feel it should be. I know I have no right to say any of this to you and maybe it is all wrong and sounds glib. We barely know one another in most ways. Yet I owe you a great debt for having, in a sense, saved my sister (as she put it to me) and hope you too can begin to look for a new life of acceptance and joy.

Sincerely,

Fred Glaysher

Searle Drive
Normal, Illinois

7 November 1989

Dear Eleanor,

I was worried my last letter would sound callow. I suppose it was. I know you're too kind to say so. Today our secular worldview so thoroughly vitiates most thinking about death. Certainly there is something right in there being a time for each of us. The old Christian theologians used to say unabashedly, unlike today, that the purpose of life is death. I think it's precisely the lack of any serious view of life and death that deprives our culture of any hope of surmounting the endless trivialities that are swiftly consuming it.

Abdul-Baha understood so well the forces tearing down the modern world. There's a statement by him in *Promulgation of Universal Peace* I often think of. In it he recognizes how thorough the secularizing influences of modernity actually are. He does so with something like a shock of recognition. I tend to connect it with his references to Voltaire in the *Secret of Divine Civilization*, written so early in his life when Nietzsche and his kind were just beginning to take flight. Of course, Bahá'u'lláh, in prophetic terms, said as much on many occasions, but, by and large, there is so very little consideration of these sobering matters by most Bahá'ís. The Guardian, though, perceived quite fully, I think, that only increasing violence and social collapse could ever result from the corrupt values that have been kneaded into the inmost soul of this century. Most Bahá'ís don't like to face that aspect of his writings, if they even read them, but I find myself ever more unable to read anything else. Abdul-Baha, of course, was largely a man of the nineteenth century, and the things written during his day by the friends are all so tainted with their dreamy and immature mysticism. Other than the Guardian there are only a few relatively recent books worth reading, and I've read over the years just about everything. He had, as Rúhíyyih Khánum says of him in her biography, "a sober, guided mind." Perhaps you view this as morose or arrogant, but, you see, I will probably live for many years to come, and am torn between my sincere belief in the Faith and my revulsion for the low intellectual and spiritual level it still operates on. I can allow that people are different but still feel quite caught between two worlds. The spiritual vacuum of the last hundred years or so has steadily driven writers and other thoughtful people further out of society. Indeed, it has destroyed any society worthy of the name. Nothing has yet evolved to a point capable of filling the void. It's painfully obvious that most Bahá'ís utterly lack the sophistication required even to perceive the situation as it truly exists. I say this all by way of clarification, not self-pity. I know somehow I have been blessed far beyond anything I deserve.

Growing up in Rochester, I fully experienced in either my own family or those of my friends, most of whom were decidedly more bourgeois than my own and who exposed me to other varieties of social corruption, all the pernicious diseases eating away at society. At times it seems to me that everything I've ever done or studied, including the Writings, had the single purpose of convincing me of the erosion of traditional American values, as well as the traditional moral values of other countries. Bahá'u'lláh said many times that it would all be swept away and no one believed him. Pam and I joke occasionally that everything I touch turns to collapse. But of course it's no joke. Firuz Kazemzadeh wrote an article in the fifties on the collapse of the traditional values of Islamic societies that evokes quite suggestively Shoghi Effendi's own meditations on the decline he observed so intently. Allowing for cultural differences and so forth, it all holds true for the rest of the globe as well. Whether in sociology, literature, or any other discipline, the verdict remains the same.

These are the things that have concerned me for years, and

the more I've studied the more I've come to realize how grave the situation actually is. I'm sure you found a much more "optimistic" reading of it all at Louhelen. I'm dumbfounded at times by how naive and uninformed, even of the Writings let alone of modern literature or history in general, most Bahá'ís are. I recognize a healthy, living religion must allow for many gradations of human capacity. But our society is ever more rabidly secular and declining ever further into immorality and depravity. I wrote the Universal House of Justice for the first time last May, so disturbed had I become by the immense disparity between the Writings and the credulous attitude most Bahá'ís have. Shoghi Effendi's post-World War II writings are so perceptive of the spiritual, political implications, and of communism, and yet most of his dire warnings go unheeded or unknown by most people in the Faith. Strange. How weak we human beings really are. So eager for vague and misty solutions. Even Abdul-Baha, writing in January of 1920, perceived the shape of things to come: "The Movement of the Left will acquire great importance. Its influence will spread" (SWA 250). That's the key passage for Shoghi Effendi too, the one he repeatedly brooded on in almost every book or collection of his letters, calling it "ominous" and "prophetic." Unfortunately most Bahá'ís know next to nothing about this aspect of the Writings and the actual, undeniably bitter history of the Soviet Union. Most tend to think apparently the Soviet Union doesn't exist or its ideology doesn't present any serious problem (since they don't know anything about it). Most seem content to reflect the confused liberal opinions of our own country without weighing them against the Writings. How different is the Guardian's sober evaluation of the USSR in *Citadel of Faith*: "a ruthless, a vigilant, a powerful and inveterate enemy" (126). How timely those words sound today—alas, they go unheeded. I have searched the Writings diligently for something comparable to the tendency today to view the US as equivalent to the USSR. Other than the condemnation of the "crass materialism" (125) of each society, there is nothing save an occasionally subtle comment. Shoghi Effendi carefully specifies the United States as "though to a lesser degree" (124).

I attended a few weeks ago the yearly Adlai E. Stevenson Memorial Lecture hosted here in town by the UNA. I usually go to such events with high hopes and leave extremely depressed. The UNA here is largely nothing other than a personality cult organized around the memory of Adlai Stevenson. It's really quite out of touch with the actual state of affairs regarding the UN and our own continuing decline of commitment to it, made official recently by the dismissing of our UN ambassador from the President's cabinet. How slow we human beings are to learn, and what short memories we have.

Thank you for your kind words on my family. There are so many dangers today, and it's getting worse all the time. I hope as the years go by we can be worthy of such praise. Incredibly, we've been told that in Elliot's elementary school somewhere between fifty and seventy percent of the children come from broken homes. The mother of one little boy in his class brazenly informed us that she had him because she just felt like it and, after seeing Ethan, would have to think about finding another man, apparently anyone would do, with which to have another child. Saul Bellow writes humorously somewhere about how we live in a time in which we are now witnessing even the breakdown of the nuclear family. You see, if one is not to delude oneself, everything turns to collapse. Normal America.

I trust you're not looking for my letters to cheer you up, because obviously that's not in my line. On the other hand I hope they don't depress you. Things are grim, but the human race is resilient, though slow to learn. I'm afraid that's as much of a hopeful flourish as I can muster at the moment.

I quite agree with you about the value of suffering. Only suffering can really open the heart and soul to God. Without it people remain somehow lacking in the deeper strains of vision and life. Historically, too, as the histories of the Old Testament, the Qur'án, the experience of early Buddhism in Japan, and so many other historical upheavals demonstrate—only immense suffering, always the result of social collapse and war, have ever truly kneaded into the soul the full implications of a new revelation. How suggestive Shoghi Effendi is on this very fact in *Messages to the Bahá'í World*. He was wrong about World War II being "the final eruption," as he called it in *Messages to America* (18). Yet, try as I might, I can't believe he's wrong about World War II being a mere "foretaste" (CF 125) of a much more devastating world war. In his history of the long conflict between ancient Sparta and Athens, Thucydides offers his work to "those inquirers who desire an exact knowledge of the past as an aid to the interpretation of the future, which in the course of human things must resemble if it does not reflect it." Today the similarity of events to ancient Greece, the long build-up to World War I, and, following the loss of commitment to the ideals of the League of Nations, World War II itself, leave little doubt, even before considering the Guardian's own writings, that another total war is in the offing. Sadly, tragically, the many treaties for peace, which preceded both major wars, meant nothing, and those who have a sense of history and are tough-minded cannot be deluded into imagining today is any different, especially when combined with a thorough reading of Soviet ideology and history.

During the last three or four years I've read almost everything of value related to the League of Nations and the United Nations—all the important addresses and writings of Woodrow Wilson, Franklin D. Roosevelt, Herbert Hoover, Winston Churchill, Dag Hammarskjöld, Charles Malik, U Thant, Adlai Stevenson, Kurt Waldheim, Brian Urquhart, and others of equal stature. I've been particularly struck by how farsighted they were (including to my surprise Hoover and Churchill) and yet how disappointing the results. One hopes of course that nothing is ever lost, but humankind seems to have learned little from the bitter history of this century. And then, as many have rightly and honestly pointed out, the Soviet Union has never had the slightest interest in developing the UN into an effective institution, and we ourselves have definitely lost all real commitment to it during the last decade or so—actually since Vietnam. How well Thucydides knew the future would resemble if not reflect the past. Charles Malik, who served on the UN commission that wrote the Universal Declaration of Human Rights, states in his book *Man in the Struggle for Peace* that what's needed is a writer who can do what Tolstoy did in *War and Peace*, but with the history of the UN, and more from the spiritual perspective of Dostoevsky. This has always struck me as most apropos. The perspective, though, must take in a much more expansive frame of time—since the Enlightenment and the French Revolution, I would say—and fully confront the social and spiritual implications of the continual secularization of the last few hundred years as well as the increasing horror of World War I and II. It would have to be a mature, Dantean work, grounded in Bahá'u'lláh's view of history. It would have to acknowledge that though evil may have no metaphysical reality, it does have existential reality; though privative, "evil exists too, and we cannot close our eyes to it, even though it is a negative existence" (*Unfolding Destiny* 458). I've always responded deeply to Abdul-Baha's succinct phrasing of this truth: "Man is a reality which stands between light and darkness" (PUP 465).

It grieves me because I know how thoroughly bankrupt Christianity is, as Bahá'u'lláh said it would become. Czeslaw Milosz, a Nobel laureate in literature, put it quite well in a recent poem: "The rule of the Galilean is ended." It amazes me that many Bahá'ís fail to realize how true this is.

Like most people I too know despair and in moments of weakness have prayed for death rather than . . . well, anyway, life is always worth living, no matter how intense the agony, loneliness, lack of companionship and understanding. Cheap and sentimental words for the young to utter. Perhaps. I trust you know I meant well with my last letter, as always. Your letters don't overwhelm me. I worry, however, that mine may overwhelm you. I don't claim to be always right but only evidence firmly grounded in the Writings and steeped in the cultural and social history of the last few hundred years could ever persuade me otherwise on many issues.

Yours,

Fred Glaysher

Searle Drive
Bloomington-Normal, Illinois

16 March 1990

Dear Elinor,

I'm ashamed to realize I've misspelled your name a couple of times. There's simply no excuse for that. All attempts to make amends aside, I must say I much prefer the proper spelling. I'm sure you do too!

During late fall and early winter I was studying several sociological studies of modern and American culture that I have always felt a need to read but had never quite gotten around to. Since late December or so I've been working my way through a long bibliography of two hundred and sixty books on the United Nations that I had compiled with the help of a computer database. I was surprised that I actually had already read most of the relevant works and have had to read only about thirty that I had missed, most of them recently published. A few have been particularly interesting—Brian Urquhart's *Decolonization and World Peace* and Carlos Romulo's *Forty Years: A Third World Soldier at the UN*. I have found most of them though to be the same old thing. Lots of talk about the UN and the necessity of world commitment and little practical recognition of the immensely intransigent nationalistic barriers to any further development of global institutions. Urquhart's book was especially interesting because, while recognizing the seeming improvements in the Soviet Union, he cautions repeatedly that we not forget their past lack of honesty and boundless capacity for deception and evil. Carlos Romulo was the Philippine ambassador to the UN for many years and the President of the General Assembly for fourteen years. I found his perspective really quite fascinating. Of the many books I've read on the UN his is the only one that marshals a knowledgeable argument from the third world for broadening the scope of the UN into a full world government. There are of course other books from third-world authors but none as persuasive as his. I really came away from it with the deep realization that, as Urquhart says somewhere else, there are many in the third world who fully understand the necessity for a world government and who may indeed have the ability to form one should the West continue down the path of self-destruction.

I am afraid I can find no reason for hope in "peace" breaking out in Europe. Quite the contrary. It seems to me we are witnessing a foolish and headlong retreat to nationalism and the dangerous notion of a balance of power—dressed up today in such fashionable euphemisms as multipolar world and the like. Roosevelt was quite right when he told Congress in 1945 after his return from Yalta that such schemes have been "tried for centuries and have always failed." There is no discussion about truly extending and improving the UN. Whatever the intentions of Gorbachev, they are quite outside the experience that brought humankind to the League of Nations and the United Nations and are grounded in the dialectic—that pernicious doctrine that all Soviet leaders have repeatedly used to such wretched ends—yet apparently few in the West remember the individual suffering of the murdered millions. And whatever our rhetoric in public may be, we continue to commit such transgressions of the UN Charter as the bombing of Libya and the invasions of Grenada and Panama—actions that further erode international restraint and stability and that further demonstrate we have lost all true commitment to the ideals of the Charter. It seems to me the Guardian was right when he told Rúhíyyíh Rabbaní, as she states in *The Priceless Pearl* (190), that it would be foolish to think another world war is not going to occur and equally foolish to think the superpowers will not use every weapon at their disposal. Alas, for the human race. I too think of the "individual suffering" involved—such abstractions about the glorious but vague future that blind many Bahá'ís to the utter horror of such upheavals means little to me any more—I suppose I've matured somewhat. Bahá'u'lláh wept over individuals. There is something inhuman about forgetting that.

I therefore can't be cheerful about the prospect of communism achieving complete domination of the globe. As a mere statement of fact, they have killed millions of individual souls. I know to a deeper level than most Bahá'ís the litany of the evils of America, but that hasn't happen here yet, nor is it a foregone conclusion that it will. Abdul-Baha states what to me is the appropriate attitude on page 250 of *Selections*:

> The Movement of the Left will acquire great importance. Its influence will spread. Strive ye, therefore, with the help of God, with illumined minds and hearts and a strength born of heaven, to become a bestowal from God to man, and to call into being for all humankind, comfort and peace.

Far from passivity and acceptance of a return to barbarism, it seems to me Abdul-Baha is here urging that Bahá'ís make the effort to bring the Faith to the attention of others as the only truly viable alternative to the false god of communism. I am reminded of Edmund Burke's famous dictum that all evil needs to triumph is for good men to do nothing. Many outside the Faith (and inside) have of course despaired of the West's ability to oppose communism in the long run and for good reason—as recent events show. Western liberalism, as Saul Bellow and many first-rate writers have pointed out, just does not have the spiritual resources to defeat it. Whether the Faith does is a matter that remains to be seen. Whittaker Chambers, who was a communist during the thirties but left the CP and eventually became a Quaker and vehement anti-communist, conceded in his book *Witness* that he had joined "the side of probable defeat." Recently, two writers who were involved with the New Left during the sixties have published a book called *Destructive Generation* that makes much the same point. I just don't share the view that it's inevitable. The Guardian's post-World War II writings do not conceive of it as such. It seems incontestable to me that his view was that a third world war would take place, causing immense destruction, but result in exactly what World War I and II did—an institution either global in nature or at least a further step in that direction. That is how I see it, bitter as it may be. From where the spark will come that will set it off, one can't predict—but the requisite volatility is quite pronounced. More so now than ever before.

In 1950 John Foster Dulles in his book *War or Peace* sounded a note of warning that I often think of:

> If at any time in the near future it seems that the danger of war has passed, that will be a period of greatest peril. Then we may be tempted to relax and get careless and disarm, materially and morally. By so doing, we should expose ourselves to a sudden attack, which is most likely to come at such a time.

In my mind I connect this passage to the Guardian's observation in *Citadel of Faith* that the full implications of Abdul-Baha's Tablet on the Movement of the Left are "as yet undisclosed" and of which "we may well anticipate, the American nation, as yet insufficiently schooled by adversity, must sooner or later experience" (37). "Insufficiently schooled by adversity" is a phrase that haunts me and leads me to believe there is much truth to the allegation of many Christian theologians that Americans are all too naive in their simple-minded longing for peace. Evil is an eternal capacity of the human soul, such theologians wisely point out, and not eradicated by mere good-intentions. It seems to me Abdul-Baha shares this tough-minded understanding of evil and the duality of human nature, though most Bahá'ís are, I think, quite childish in their understanding of him, partly, I suppose, because they have never read the scripture and best literature that deal with the nature of evil. I am not arguing for original sin but for recognition of the reality of man's eternal capacity for evil and sin—as well as good. Such recognition counsels the utmost caution and circumspection dealing with those who have established a long and irrefutable record of evil. And of course it counsels humble acceptance of our own fallibility and potential for evil. I quite agree with those who say the modern era has produced such appalling atrocities partially because it has repudiated the reality of light and darkness. Voltaire and Rousseau were among the first writers to claim man was entirely good and free of all limitations. Oh, what sad results that notion has produced.

Richard Nixon reveals in his autobiography *1999: Victory without War* what our national leaders truly think:

> What moves the world for good or ill is power, and no sovereign nation will give up its power to the UN or any other body—not now and not ever. This is an immutable aspect of national character (50).

The similarity of thinking to Nietzsche is breathtaking. There can be little doubt that Ronald Reagan and George Bush also share this tragic prejudice, as do the leaders of other nations. It seems to me inescapable that the path leading from Richard Nixon's credo to Bahá'u'lláh's passes through the valley of the shadow of death. We have already seen twice in this century that nothing else but total war has the capacity to transform the views of power-hungry nihilists and inspire them to rise above their nationalistic fetishes. What the Guardian called a "tempest" and "judgment of God." He Alone is the Lord of history and the Mover of the world. Nixon's "victory without war" is essentially a return to a cynical balance of power.

Too often we Bahá'ís dream about the glory of the vague future and do too little to bring it about. I don't have any gift for or interest in administration, but if I do have any ability or purpose whatsoever, it's at least to try to articulate in literary form the truth of the Bahá'í revelation in such a way that it will appeal to the imagination of those who are the most thoughtful and knowledgeable about the best in the cultural past. I believe

I've written three books that move in that direction and hope that somehow I will eventually find a publisher for them and be allowed to write what I feel, after many years of perseverance and arduous study, is still my major ambition.

A month or so ago I attended a conference at the University of Chicago sponsored by the Intercollegiate Studies Institute. They publish the journal *Modern Age*, in which I've published a few essays. They are very conservative and Catholic. They tend to flirt with a return to the thirteenth century—Thomistic philosophy. Unlike liberal and Marxist publications today, they at least believe in God, have some sense of the social and moral degradation consequent to the loss of religious belief, and a mature, tragic sense of history, though I don't agree with their interpretation of it. Of course they are as reactionary as could be. Or in most respects. Especially in their deification of the American past, as largely concocted by them since 1950. It may come as no surprise that they claim they laid the intellectual foundation, if it can be called that, for the postwar conservative movement. Basically monarchist to proto-fascist leanings, willing to settle for any type of conservative autarchy. The more sober and subtle intellects among them, however, realize, as one of them wrote a few years ago, as a nation "we have already passed the point of no return." The better minds also realize Catholicism is definitely defunct. The theme of the conference was "Is the Soviet Threat Over?" Unlike the credulous elements of the Western media (which Andrei Sakharov claimed in 1978 were already firmly committed to Marxism) or Bahá'ís who have never read Shoghi Effendi's sober letters, they at least were responsible enough to answer that question intelligently. But blinded by their deluded worship of the nation-state and capitalism.

After leaving that event shaking my head, I attended a few days later another UNA lecture—one on global ecology. It was an interesting lecture, from which I learned a lot. Beyond the generalities of the green house effect one picks up from the news, I knew very little about it. Of course, in terms of a truly informed scientific understanding, I still don't, but I do have a much deeper impression of the severity of the situation and its potential for causing widespread collapse and commotion. I won't try to rehearse such details as three to five foot rises in the ocean, perhaps no matter what we do now, and perhaps nineteen to thirty feet if we do nothing. What struck me was that given the considerable knowledge of the global scale of the problem, both the audience and the lecturer (a professor of biology at Wesleyan) could only conceive of action being taken in terms of the nation-state. When I asked the speaker whether he thought adequate measures could be taken in time outside the framework of a world government and whether he could think of any instance in which the nation-states had the will to work effectively on such an immensely complex problem, I quickly became aware that I had sounded a note of reality no one wanted to hear—even at a UNA meeting (a cynic might say especially).

I appreciate the clipping on Robert Hayden. I have always had ambivalent feelings regarding him and his work and am reluctant to say too much in a letter. I owe him a great deal. It was primarily out of that recognition that I edited his prose and poems since I knew there was no one else who could have properly done the job, given the taste of some concerned. Anyone else would have produced volumes that would have been the death blow to his reputation—heavily annotated and academic texts. It's kind of you to say his work is powerful, but, between the two of us, I've always been pained by its minor qualities. He doesn't do and never even attempted what major writers do. He begrudgingly recognized that. Of course his work is, nevertheless, on an intelligent level and far, far beyond what any other Bahá'í has ever achieved. He was a good man and an excellent poet.

I must say, though, that when I heard of the little event being arranged at Louhelen by the individual involved I could only feel seething contempt for her. I remember hearing from Robert Hayden how at Bahá'í Feast shortly after he had been to the

Carter White House and given a reading there this person's "Persian" husband had the temerity to go far out of his way to insult him by asking if any Bahá'í had done anything to teach the Faith recently, while glaring at him. Reading at The White House apparently wasn't on a low enough level for the philistine. I regret that I missed that Feast. But I had and have seen many others like it. How revealing of human nature that this person's spouse, who always operated on the same crude and banal level, had the gall to exploit his reputation for a negligible little propaganda event. Bob told me once what he thought of her: "She's so gun-ho it's sickening."

I've experienced this same Philistinism in the Faith many times. As elsewhere. I've always realized that I had to publish in intellectually respectable circles for it to amount to anything. Within merely Bahá'í circles it's like throwing it down a rat hole. I recently had an amusing confirmation of this. Nevertheless, I remained open to the possibility for a long time that perhaps for truly new and challenging literary work to be done, it might just have to come from outside predominant circles—through Bahá'í sources. I therefore kept a close eye out, so to speak, for any sign that something might be developed enough somewhere to be worth investigating. My experience, though, has been that usually the various little Bahá'í publishers and organizations can't even properly respond to a simple letter of query let alone edit and correctly publish something on an intelligent level. I won't go into all the risible details of my attempting to deal with a Bahá'í publisher in England, but, suffice it to say, my work proved to be so far beyond them it was pitiful. Ah, despair. A very lonely feeling. I am thankful I knew Robert Hayden and heard from him so often, "Why I continue to have anything to do with Bahá'ís, I do not know, I do not know." Oddly enough, it gives me strength to think of that at times. Perhaps he knew it would eventually.

Thank God though for human diversity, and that at its best this religion can unite very different people.

I was sadden to hear of your fiftieth wedding anniversary and thought of your not having Bob there. I'm very sorry. Such things shouldn't be. Why God permits them I just don't know. The Old Testament and Jewish theology in general may be more perceptive and healthy in this respect than Christianity and the Bahá'í Faith thus far. I'm thinking particularly of the Book of Job and elsewhere when God is denounced to His face for allowing suffering beyond what human beings can understand in this world. And I thought selfishly about Pam. Sometimes it's hard for me to believe we've been married already for ten years. I don't know what I'd ever do emotionally and spiritually if anything happened to her. I love her so much and truly can't imagine life without her. We are quite grateful that we have been given one another and, though it may sound trite, two wonderful children as well.

I apologize for the length of this letter. Please don't feel you have to burden yourself by responding to the same length or at all. I'd feel bad if you're wearing yourself out just to answer my grim letters.

I'm glad to hear you feel a change in your healing from your loss of Bob. I'm very thankful to hear that. Thank God that though grief never disappears it can become easier to bear. And that of course doesn't imply any diminution of affection for the loved one, quite the contrary.

Searle Drive
Normal, Illinois

17 May 1990

Dear Elinor,

I hope you don't moan at the sight of another letter from me in your mailbox! It seems that you have known me, if only from afar, long enough that I can feel comfortable in writing to you about matters most other Bahá'ís wouldn't understand or have the proper perspective on. Perhaps you'd prefer if I didn't! I don't know. I hope you understand my putting into words what is too often left unsaid in Bahá'í circles, too often left unconfronted and therefore unconsidered, and affairs continue to drift for lack of recognition of the way things truly are. The Faith is really at such a primitive stage of development.

I attended National Convention at the House of Worship this year and was once again struck by that fact. It was the first Convention here in the US I have ever attended. I went to one in Japan, but it was very small, about fifty people, mostly foreigners, a dozen or maybe two dozen Japanese Bahá'ís. This year's Convention was on a small scale too, of course. Just enough to fill Foundation Hall, almost. Although I've attended District Convention in Michigan and down here, I was fascinated at how it actually went. Have you ever been to the National Convention?

The most important class I had at the University of Michigan, even more so, in a sense, than studying with Robert Hayden, was one with a Christian scholar, George Mendenhall, on the social thought of the Old Testament prophets. He wrote a brilliant book, *The Tenth Generation*, on the collapse of Mediterranean and Judaic civilization during the Late Bronze Age and thereafter. Of the many classes I've had in my life, his is the only one that I have found myself continually going back to, reconsidering my notes, rereading, and so forth. Primarily of course it's due to the profundity of the Biblical text itself. It so clearly records the collapse of civilization, repeatedly and over many generations, when, as Bahá'u'lláh says, "The vitality of men's belief in God is dying out," and all the sundry social dislocations that result. The *Qur'án* and the *Kitáb-I-Iqán* embrace a similar historical view, but both are much more poetic and succinct than the Old Testament. The Old Testament is so full of marvelous details.

At times I feel something like kinship with St. Augustine, who had entirely let go of the Roman world, its cults, factions, and ideologies. I had a two-semester course in Roman history at the University of Michigan that also figures significantly somehow into my being and that gave me a very thorough treatment of the late Roman empire and all its ills, though I had also had a brief survey course earlier. The professor typically laid all the blame on economic reasons and derided all attempts to introduce the moral interpretation Christianity has always held of the collapse of Rome. I remember one Catholic fellow who strenuously tried to interject some element of sanity into the discussion only to be beaten down with the usual liberal clichés. Arnold Toynbee mentions in one of his books that up to 1914 no one at Oxford was very much concerned with the history of the late Roman empire, but, after that year, he and others were quite overwhelmed by the similarity of events. I have often wondered if the Guardian did not imbibe such a sober perspective at Oxford, though of course he had studied Roman history earlier in Beirut. Certainly by 1936 he had recognized the Roman analogy:

> Must the inauguration of so vast, so unique, so illumined an era in human history be ushered in by so great a catastrophe in human affairs as to recall, nay surpass, the appalling collapse of Roman civilization in the first centuries of the Christian Era? (WOB 202)

Similarly in 1957 in *Messages to the Bahá'í World* (104) the Guardian mentioned how "the process of progressive deterioration" recalled "the convulsions which, on a far more restricted scale, seized a declining empire in the opening centuries of the Christian era."

Of course one must guard against a shallow apocalyptic mentality that exaggerates the eternally woeful condition of humankind into something much more terminal than it in fact is.

The ecological apocalypticism I mentioned in my last letter is the kind of thing I feel many reservations about since it may, at least to some degree, reflect a hidden political agenda rather than scientific fact. Nevertheless, outside the Faith, and some might say even within it, there is so very little to be hopeful about in the near future.

I quite agree with you about the "hucksters wanting to use all the modern sales" approaches in teaching the Faith. I think I can understand why you'd say it has gotten worse. I used to think there was a place for more of that than I do now and find it exceedingly repulsive, though I recognize on an intellectual level that all religions in the past required a popular form that could appeal to the masses before they began to spread widely throughout society. Buddhism in Japan is a particularly good example of this phenomenon. It's difficult, though, to accept the mindless emotional enthusiasm that passes among some for the Bahá'í Faith and the Machiavellian calculation of others. And yet human nature is indeed diverse.

Have you decided yet to make plans to move to the Quaker retirement community you mentioned? I hope your children can help you with that. I'm sure Bob must have handled all that kind of thing and would hate to see you taken advantage of by some unethical operation. Occasionally one hears reports on the news and so forth that are really quite alarming, and we have naturally thought of you. I trust you have a good lawyer who can advise you too, just to be careful. I would think your brother's experience would be the most reliable guide in assessing what you might expect to find living there actually like.

I hope your environmental allergies are giving you some respite, though I suppose this must be the difficult season.

Searle Drive
Bloomington-Normal, Illinois

21 July 1990

Dear Elinor,

I am surprised somewhat to hear you've decided not to move to the Quaker retirement community. You seemed to think so highly of it. I suppose you are probably right about the difficulty of fitting into the regimen of group living, the buildings, and so forth. I can understand too that you would be giving up a lot by moving from your home of so many years.

Your letter led to thoughts on many things, but I hesitate to plunge into it all. I worry that I am taking up more of your time than I should, given your other demands. You must be more candid about this matter if our correspondence is too much of a strain. I certainly wouldn't think less of you if it were. And I hope you don't misunderstand my mentioning this or feel hurt by it. I am just worried that my own need to put things into writing might blind me to your own priorities. You needn't feel obligated to respond within any specific span of time. A leisurely approach is best for both of us.

Your mentioning the drug scene made me think of a recent conversation I had with a friend of mine who works on the Chicago Commodities Exchange. He grew up in Rochester too, in Great Oaks. I stayed with him and his wife in Evanston when I attended National Convention. Over dinner one night I was relating to them the fact that Elliot's elementary school has a drug program for fifth and sixth-graders because there are children in his school who are actually already using drugs. Their response to my fear and concern for my own child and others was that, well, drugs exist, and they're a problem, and you just gotta be aware of them, and there's nothing you can do about it. They are good people, but I was appalled at their complete inability to perceive the immense threat the drug scene truly represents to our entire society. My attempt to try to convey that fact to them met with only dismissive incredulity and that was after his telling me how every time he goes into the restroom at the Commodities Exchange he sees five or six brokers, some of whom are making more than half a million dollars a year, "snorting" cocaine.

I've been reading this spring the work of an Italian philosopher and jurist, Giambattista Vico. He wrote a superb book on the "rise, development, maturity, decline, and fall" of nations from a Catholic perspective, in about 1744. It's a fascinating book because he comes late enough to take into account such political philosophers as Machiavelli and yet still early enough to retain an unsentimental religious perspective. Marx twisted his work for his own purposes and other communists often cite him as an early source for the decline of monarchies and capitalism and the eventual triumph of the proletariat. (I had a Marxist professor at U of M who relished the irony of perverting Vico.)

Oswald Spengler, who wrote *The Decline of the West* (1918), with which Shoghi Effendi seems to have had some familiarity, and Arnold Toynbee to a degree, secularize Vico and dress up his ideas in proto-fascist or liberal guise. Vico has an unusually penetrating understanding of the barbarism society has fallen prey to in the past and its eternal potential for collapse. The uncanny predictive ability of the prophetic tradition is the result of its being based on transcendent moral principles which eventually always prove their veracity through historical decline. It would seem to be a primordial or archetypal religious truth. One our society lost long, long ago. Societies always breakdown for a multitude of reasons.

Ibn Khaldun was an early Islamic historian who has much in common with Vico. I first learned of him in a few courses I had at U of M in Islamic studies. Ibn Khaldun wrote on the decline of Berber and Arabic civilization during the 14th century. His emphasis is that the hedonistic stage of a society leads to a loss of will and fortitude and people lose the ability to sacrifice and share. As this process deepens there's a loss of solidarity or group feeling—brotherhood in a sense. Everyone is pitted against everyone else. Society fragments. He traces these changes to the loss of a moral purpose or telos—in short, unifying transcendent belief. It's always the same. Ecclesiastes got it right. There is nothing new under the sun. Daniel Bell, a sociologist of modern and American culture, has elucidated throughout his work how destructive of social cohesion the materialistic values of capitalism are—that capitalism itself is undermining the preconditions necessary for its own existence by inculcating a self-indulgent ethos, through its advertising, among other ways. All the best sociologists have said something like this, Max Weber for instance, at the beginning of the century. Usually their perspective tends to socialism but their basic critique is somewhat congruent with a religious view, though many wouldn't agree.

It is a sad fact that religion has been leaching out of education for a very long time, which is only to say out of our society, all societies. I have ambivalent feelings about it. In one sense I say good riddance to the narrow mentality and bigotry that always wraps itself in nationalistic garb, no matter what nation. Spiritually and intellectually the religions are quite enervated. In another sense I believe religious belief is quite essential for scholarship or creative work of any truly humane and sane quality to result. Vico repeats the well-known fact that for most of the Greek philosophers and writers divine providence was the fundamental tenet one had to hold prior to serious discussion. It's all gone though in the modern world. It's been pouring out of all the cracks in the modern soul for decades, if not a couple of centuries.

You mention books on the Sufis and St. John of the Cross. I've read many such works, especially Rumi, long ago. I value them highly and can understand why you'd respond to them, but, really, they don't mean much any more. They belong to antiquated religions, to past dispensations. They are like artifacts from an ancient civilization cast up on some lonely and barren shore where no one quite knows what to make of them. All the religions have been reduced to detritus, as Bahá'u'lláh so often said they would. There are, of course, interesting cultural curios that aesthetes revere, or those of us who admire aspects of the past, but, to me, little more remains. The modern soul has different preferences. One of my professors made the difference blatantly clear to me when he derisively asked me, "Do you think anybody cares about your and Hayden's religion?" Other than a few professors I had in Christian and Islamic studies, I never had anyone at U of M who felt anything other than vehement contempt for religion, including the Bahá'í Faith. So what you mention does not surprise me. What surprises me is that so few Bahá'ís understand the way things truly stand in the university—well, come to think of it, that doesn't really surprise me.

Today, if one is a Marxist, or some other type of radical with violent leanings, one can expect much help and encouragement—I saw it repeatedly at U of M—at the least, exceedingly formalistic beliefs are required, which shut out all forms of transcendent belief, especially when I was there. Down here at this excuse for a university the Marxists just recently gained considerably more power in the English department. It's happening everywhere. The loss of belief in God always leads eventually to some form of oppression—what Toynbee liked to call man-worship.

Mark Tobey wrote an insightful letter about the role of art and about Bahá'ís that I think of at times:

> As you well know the Guardian freed art from didactic purposes. 'There is no official Bahá'í art.' I think it would always be best if the Bahá'ís would show they like art—respect it—it would be impressive to those non-Bahá'ís who are interested in art. This would be enough and a more rightful way.

He wrote this letter to the NSA at a time when Bahá'ís were attempting to exploit his work for some cheap little propaganda event—that is, they didn't have the slightest respect or interest in it as art—for its spiritual vision—but merely as an occasion for publicity for their own ulterior motives. Robert Hayden often went through this too. He told me of an incident when he was giving a poetry reading in Wilmette, one which he related to many people. The Bahá'í "administrator" who was sent to pick him up at the airport asked him "And what have you done to serve the Faith?" Clearly nothing on a low and ignorant enough level to suit his risible tastes. This is very difficult for Bahá'ís who actually know very little about art to understand. So often the philistine mentality one meets with in many Iranian Bahá'ís, who know and respect so little about the history of the cultural development of the Western world, not to mention usually even the Middle-Eastern, seems to dominate thinking about art in the Faith. The problem is that so little of merit has been done—everything is still at such a primitive level. Bahá'u'lláh deserves more than propaganda. This situation is not solely the problem of artists for it is the result partly of the spiritual vacuum that has been opened up by modern bourgeois culture, from the most plebeian and popular forms to the most sophisticated. Artists alone cannot resolve it. It's symbolic of much deeper spiritual issues.

I've been reading recently Thomas Mann's *Doctor Faustus*. Mann was more sensitive than perhaps any other artist in this century to the spiritual implications of the loss of respect for the artist and the increasing expectation that the artist be a propagandist for the state, as under Hitler and Stalin. Of course in Western countries serious art has increasingly been swept aside by shallow materialistic contempt for anything that can't be eaten or deposited in a bank. Someone wrote somewhere or another that in the modern world the religions have all given up the search for truth but it has been passed to the artist. There is a sense in which this is true. By and large modern artists, and I mean the best artists, the ones with a real calling, have spoken the truth, as they should, but, as Mann and others point out, the truth is not pretty in this century and the people don't want to hear it. They prefer lies, as they always have. I'm afraid Bahá'ís reflect this same shortcoming. They want propaganda that will help build up, so they think, the new world order and don't care whatsoever about truth, which is art's burden and glory. As they say, it takes all kinds, and many are now clamoring to provide what the undiscerning majority want. It's on a quite pitiful level though, and will never appeal to an intellect of any quality whatsoever or earn any real respect for the Faith. It seems to me sophisticated Bahá'ís realize much of this and there have been a few things published recently that seem to understand that serious work probably won't fare any better with Bahá'ís than it has ever usually fared in prevailing circles.

Mann rightly views the ever-increasing isolation and decline of art as a result of the attempt to substitute art for religious belief, with which I agree. It is a reflection of the contempt of the modern world for spirituality, the non-material, in any form. Again, in so far as that is true, the solution, if you will, provided there's one, lies partly outside the realm of the artist—society itself must change sufficiently to recognize the spiritual validity of the critique of art in the modern world; that is, it's negative message for the last hundred years or so. By expressing revulsion with the spiritual banality and materialism that pervade modern society, artists have been honest and loyal to their calling. To do anything else at this stage of history would be to mouth sugar-coated lies. Lies will never earn respect for the Faith nor attempts to coerce artists into doing so. It seems to me many Bahá'ís seem to conceive of the role of the artist as court jester or lackey. The Soviet debasement of art to the crudest level of gross propaganda comes to mind. Such people are largely well-meaning—they want to see the Faith grow, etc., as we all do. But they don't seem to perceive there are very profound issues at stake of which they apparently know nothing. Pretending they don't exist, writing in a never, never land of peace and bliss detached from all reality, will not have the effect they claim to want. It will only cause others to feel contempt for the Faith, which surely those at U of M who actually know what Robert Hayden often thought of the Faith must feel now after recent Bahá'í attempts to exploit and whitewash his work. He told me often what he thought too, after carefully closing the door of his study so that Mrs. Hayden wouldn't hear. Most of his views and problems aren't mine, but if we shared anything as friends, it was a commitment to truth. Honesty requires nothing less.

You mention the need for intellectuals and I suppose you're referring to the Universal House of Justice's Ridvan Message. The whole modern notion of intellectuals evolved with the loss of religious belief during the Enlightenment and has often had very dire results. It's a commonplace that intellectuals prepared the way in their writings for such bloodbaths as the French Revolution, the Soviet debacle, and Hitler. Many point out the parallel to what is happening in American universities today. I feel much like Thomas Mann's character Tonio Kröger, who had little respect for such so-called intellectuals and artists and who yet was no more at home with the bourgeoisie whom he regarded as a far-off form of humanity, as Rilke put it, but at least respected them more so. I don't know though, I can and do accept that not everyone feels so intensely as I do about all these things, but I've never been able to understand how most can settle for so little. I remember friends' homes in Great Oaks and Tienken Manor, how spiritually and intellectually vacuous they were, as was my own. At the time I had little understanding of why, but I knew intuitively something was deeply wrong and that with time, study, self-sacrifice, and, though I don't intend any grandiose claims, with the grace of God, I might somehow come to understand it a little more. I learned recently that one of my friends from Great Oaks who stole thousands of dollars during high school from his job as an assistant manager at a cinema and who through manipulating the legal system largely pinned it on another friend is now working for General Dynamics—difficult not to read more into that. All levels and classes of our society have become so corrupt it's terribly alarming. The historical record of many civilizations shows recovery does not come easily or painlessly but often requires a couple of hundred years and vast upheavals. I do believe Shoghi Effendi came increasingly to see it this way, as is evidenced in his later writings.

But I seem to have gotten off the track. I used to believe there was a place in the Faith for artists and intellectuals—that must be what is at least partly behind "people of capacity." I suppose that was one of the reasons I was attracted to the Faith as a young person. Many things are claimed or implied in the Writings. I find much of it extremely difficult to believe anymore. My actual experience has been very different. Robert Hayden had a good understanding of the situation. He told me once in regard to Bahá'ís, "You should make them pay for it. They'll never have any respect for it otherwise." At the time I thought he was being too hard on Bahá'ís. I no longer think so.

I highly doubt a return to an agrarian society, on the Roman model. People would have to forget far too much for that to happen—far too much would have to be wiped out and the world has become too interdependent for a thorough breakdown of communication ever to occur again, yet it is true as Kurt Waldheim writes in one of his books, and others have warned, that several hundred million people could easily be destroyed—a mere fact of available technology. It seems to me what George Orwell and others feared is more probable than a complete reversion to isolated subsistence farming: an oppressive world-state controlling all or most of the world's resources for very evil purposes. Even that, though, is to me usually less likely than a third world war or catastrophe, with vast devastation, resulting in a largely beneficent world-state that advances on the experience of the League and UN. One can't say precisely how it might come about, but I think either the millions have died for utterly nothing during this century or we are still hurtling along to another dreadful event that will force world-leaders somehow to return to a responsible understanding of our experience and to create a more effective form of global cooperation. To me the resurfacing of nationalistic passions in Eastern Europe and elsewhere is quite reminiscent of the animosities that preceded both world wars and found an outlet in such violence as the Balkan wars and Hitler's obscene glorification of the Volk. Some of our political leaders appear to have actually deluded themselves into believing they can "manage" the new "dynamic situation," as I heard it recently called. I have always remembered the words of the head of Hitler's propaganda apparatus. He informed an interviewer, "We soon discovered that if we said something long enough people would begin to believe it was true." Euphoria is one of the modern secular world's favorite recurrent narcotics. The basic features of what Shoghi Effendi called "this tragic world-engulfing conflict" have not changed or found a political form at a higher level of unity. No one is even suggesting the latter. Try as I might, I can't believe anything but that the West is woefully underestimating the danger and insidious intentions of existing Soviet capabilities and is foolishly grasping again at the liberal delusion that man can rationally control historical and social forces—a conceit that comes right out of the French Revolution and that, at its worst, has led to many disastrous attempts at social engineering.

The lesson we have yet to learn from the ever-increasing moral collapse of all countries is that secular liberalism, which the West has spread throughout the world, just does not work for long because it operates on borrowed spiritual capital, if you will. That is, as many have said, it relies on the moral leftovers of past religions and as these decline that small portion becomes less and less with every passing year. Of course we all still cling to many of the shards of liberalism, I know I do, both perhaps consciously and unconsciously, even though Shoghi Effendi warned against "excessive liberalism." Liberal-democratic thinking permeates everything I've ever read, the intellectual environment itself. But the presuppositions of liberalism are secular to the core, at best neutral, which leaves society defenseless against more militant, irrational ideologies that are quite eager to fill the vacuum. It seems to me this is why the whole experiment to create an effective League and UN has failed. It is based solely on the rationalism of the Enlightenment thinkers. Those like Nietzsche who retain a primitive and passionate devotion to the acquisition of power are much more self-sacrificing and determined than those who advocate the reasonable arguments of the founders of both organizations. Bahá'u'lláh speaks somewhere of transmuting Satanic power into heavenly strength. This is what liberalism lacks and why it always seems to give way to barbarism, whether in the university, Weimar Germany, or elsewhere. There are many signs that American democracy is exceedingly weak now too. I grieve about that fact because I love this country, have read a lot of American history and literature, and there is much that is good in Western civilization, as both Bahá'u'lláh and Shoghi Effendi testified at times. There have been many Christian writers who have pointed out for more than thirty or forty years that the Enlightenment values are dead and we are in the midst of a change as momentous as the one from the Medieval world to the Renaissance. I believe of course that that change will increasingly have to take a Bahá'í form, not a Christian one. Recently I received a letter from a liberal Christian magazine to which I had submitted an essay. They complained that I had been too hard on the Soviet Union (they conceded the Gulag was an unpleasant fact) and not hard enough on the US, though I had gone far off the subject to point to numerous defects in Western society. Their criticism didn't surprise me in the least. What did was that I cited various passages and so forth that argued that Christianity was defunct, and that they could accept without batting an eye, so indubitable to them was its truth, but failure to say a sufficient number of derogatory things about the US, well, that couldn't be tolerated! It reminded me of certain Bahá'ís.

Vico has marvelous insight into how divine providence, as he likes to say, restores order in a decaying culture:

> Hence peoples who have reached this point . . . are sensible no longer of comforts, delicacies, pleasures, and pomp, but only of the sheer necessities of life. And the few survivors . . . become sociable and, returning to the primitive simplicity of the first world of peoples, are again religious, truthful, and faithful. Thus providence brings back among them the piety, faith, and truth which are the natural foundations of justice as well as the graces and beauties of the eternal order of God.

I find this in harmony with Shoghi Effendi's descriptions of the decline of the old world order and the gradual rise of the new. Shoghi Effendi's emphasis on virtue and verities, unknown really in liberalism which leaves that up to the individual to try to figure out for himself, an arduous struggle for which few have the stamina, meshes quite well with Vico's understanding that "religions alone can bring peoples to do virtuous works by appeal to their feelings, which alone move men to perform them." It's this irrational appeal to what is best in man, since he cannot escape his dualistic nature and will either worship God or some idol, the evil side of his own being, that seems to me to have lost its force in all the religions. It deeply saddens me that the remedy seems to lie only through horrible suffering, but, in my better moments, I hope I can find solace in trust in the ultimate goodness of divine providence. Though like Job and the Jewish tradition, I believe one can say anything to God as long as it is in the defense of his creation. It seems to me that this has been a century that once again has brought us to that spiritual ash-heap. We live on it now though most of us are unable to see it clearly.

I'm not sure what you had in mind with the copied material you sent me since you don't say anything about it. The article on the "tragic age" makes me think of how rare real tragic sense is in our society. I am very fond of Sophocles' tragedy and Shakespeare's, both of whom, of course, knew what tragedy is, unlike what passes for it today. Many have said a truly tragic sense is contingent on some type of transcendent belief and with its disappearance the ability even to perceive real tragedy has also waned during the last three or four hundred years. I do believe the Writings have a very mature sense of the tragedy of life. In a way I would say the sole purpose of Bahá'u'lláh's revelation is to restore the realization that life is tragic. Most cultures have had this insight in one way or another though expressed in different ways and with varying emphasis. It's always a decadent age that forgets it. Herbert Hoover in his book *The Ordeal of Woodrow Wilson* (1958), an important book to me, though I don't share his belief that communist countries should have been kept out of the UN, suggests that with Wilson's failure a Greek-like tragedy overtook the entire modern world. Kurt Waldheim makes much the same point about the failure of the UN. I am reminded too that there is no greater tragedy than that God should send his manifestation to the world only to be ignored.

I find a complete lack of tragic sense in the June 24 Feast letter. It claims the Guardian wrote in a particular letter of "the adoption of accords to establish the Lesser Peace by the leaders of the world." Supposedly "That is being taken care of." In the passage by the Guardian, though, there is not the slightest reference to accords. He was too intelligent to imagine the Lesser Peace would ever come about in that way, unlike some of our "administrators." One can well understand how some can end in cynicism, like your friends you mentioned, given the lack of honest intelligent discussion in the Faith. What perhaps is occurring though, as reflected in the Ridvan Message, is that the paucity of "people of capacity" in the Faith is making itself felt in ways that can no longer be ignored. The Faith is in danger of being banalized out of existence.

I've witnessed this too in the way a couple of the Bahá'í magazines operate—despite their pretensions to a high intellectual level, laughable, really. And all the more laughable is their subtle clinging to the basic intellectual paradigms of modernism instead of taking seriously the revelation of

Bahá'u'lláh. There must be some way that tough-minded diversity of thought and criticism can be integrated into the Faith without accusing the person of heresy. The alternative seems to be a religion that appeals only to ignorant people. This is I suppose somewhat the kind of thing you had in mind that most Bahá'ís can't discuss without becoming upset. To me this lack of self-criticism is one of the biggest blocks to further development of the Faith. Criticism presupposes a desire to see something improve—literature, art, etc., and is all we human beings have for trying out, if you will, possible courses of thought and action. Without it we are little better than slaves of the status quo or thralls of some authoritarian's *ex cathedra* pronouncements. It should go without saying that no one is infallible. The Báb banned all non-Bábí books and people from his commonwealth, Abdul-Baha prophesied the Lesser Peace in 1957 or before the end of the twentieth century, and Shoghi Effendi certainly erred at times. I don't believe we need to lie about these things or attempt to conceal them as has been done in the past.

There are many other incidents you are perhaps aware of. I've seen over the years many sad things happen within the Faith. One of the most disturbing to me was a "prominent" Bahá'í and member of the District Teaching Committee taking a young woman to bed shortly after she declared. She isn't of course blameless, far from it, but it is understandable that she would have become disillusioned with the Faith rather quickly after that. It's the lack of mechanisms and internal criticism to deal with such things as these that worries me the most about the Faith. That and the gullibility of so many Bahá'ís. I suppose one other thing that really worries me about the Faith is the cynicism of those in the administration who eagerly use simple and sometimes young people and then sneer behind their backs—or to their faces, and I've seen it. I remember one Persian family in particular. None of the children were Bahá'ís so disaffected had they become by what they observed in their own parents over the years. The father couldn't understand why. I heard one of the children said all the parents cared about was money and impressing other Bahá'ís. At times I almost forget there are people who choose to live on that low level.

I've just finished reading *The Conservators* (1983) by Elliott Roosevelt. I find much of it quite hard to take. I won't go into all the details but it's the same old tiresome liberalism of his books on his mother and father. There is very little thought about how deep our problems really are—typical of the liberal mentality. Of course there is good in American liberalism, as in aspects of the conservative side of the spectrum, but, both are so one-sided and entrenched, they're really quite exhausted.

I was interested in his fourteen recommendations for reforming the UN. I find his suggestion for the creation of a UN force of five million men and the abolition of the veto the most important ones. Unfortunately, it will surely require catastrophe before we are willing to take those steps, which many have urged for decades. Wise men and women urged them at the San Francisco Conference, and earlier, to no avail.

I've also just finished *From the League to the UN* (1948), a collection of addresses and essays from throughout the preceding twenty years by Gilbert Murray, who realized to a surprising extent that the UN would never fulfill the hopes many people had for it precisely because of the veto and the lack of an armed force. I don't know anything about his interest in the Bahá'í Faith but apparently he contributed to a relief fund, as did Toynbee, for Persian Bahá'ís during the fifties. He was a classicist at Oxford and for many years director of the British League of Nations Union, the equivalent of the UNA. He demonstrates an exceedingly fine sensitivity to the social and intellectual decline of Western civilization from the Victorian age to the second world war. I think it's highly likely that Shoghi Effendi knew something of his work. His long historical view seems to have fortified him with less blind faith than Elliott Roosevelt in the ability of Western democratic liberalism to meet the challenges of the twentieth century. The strength with which he looks at the facts is really quite impressive. Despite a certain amount of optimistic rhetoric he appears to concede that the new "League" is ill-equipped to prevent a further descent into barbarism.

How right Bahá'u'lláh was that peace ultimately had to involve unified military might—what Shoghi Effendi called "international Force"—his capitalization and attempt to draw attention to the realistic side of the Writings. Few books on world government are as profound as Gilbert Murray's. These days most are dry technical manuals that have lost the vitality of his vision and the moral and social background requisite to understanding why world government is important in the first place. I feel it is one of those rare books that will take me a long time to absorb—one worth the effort.

Pam used to date the son of a South American Persian counselor. His son's favorite book was Machiavelli—a fact I have always found sobering since I witnessed a sanctimonious performance by him once at a Bahá'í conference at the University of Chicago, and the maudlin response of other Bahá'ís. The puerile understanding of Abdul-Baha's statements on the non-existence of evil would seem to leave many without any spiritual protection, in a sense, against what is the worst in human nature. This weakness comes right out of Islam and can be found in the work of Rumi, for instance, who completely failed to confront the reality of evil. He comments somewhere that we should just ignore it and essentially pretend it doesn't exist. A fact I would say that goes a long way toward explaining the rise to power of such Middle-Eastern despots as Ayatollah Khomeini. No Western writer could ever accept such an attitude toward evil, and I don't believe Abdul-Baha did either. There are very few safeguards in the Faith against such individuals. There is a letter written on behalf of the Guardian that addresses this concern somewhat, but I find it unconvincing:

> If an individual ostentatiously places himself in the public eye with the seeming purpose of getting people to vote for him, the members of the electorate regard this as

> self-conceit and are affronted by it; they learn to distinguish between someone who is well-known as an unintentional result of active public service and someone who makes an exhibition of himself merely to attract votes (January, 1923).

Usually it works this way. And I have seen it work. But what of that evil individual, history is largely the story of his deeds, who is not so ostentatious and does not make an exhibition of himself? What happens when it is not an "unintentional result" but coldly calculated and insidious? I have seen this type of thing in the Faith. It's quite frightening and goes a long way toward explaining why Shoghi Effendi concedes in one of his letters that the Faith too will one day degenerate, though in a way different from past religions and governments. And then what are we, therefore, to make of human nature?

I hope you understand my motives for saying these things. So often one is relegated beyond the pale for any remotely honest observation. A cause for deep concern, I would say.

I like what you say about accepting that the only one we can change is ourselves—and that even is difficult and slow, at best. Surely we're drowning under a sea of theories and abstractions about what needs to be changed and how to do it, all of which amounts to very little and which these days tends increasingly to violence and social engineering. The truth that a change of heart must begin with the individual finds very few exponents today. It's much easier to hate and revile others, and of course not one of us is innocent in this regard. We all have our little passions and prejudices, our preconceptions about what others should be and do. One likes to think the Bahá'í Faith will help to moderate this type of thing, but I have seen little proof of it, though the Writings are full of claims to the contrary, as they are about so many things, much of which has now been conveniently postponed into the vague future. It's only experience that counts. We all talk about love and are failures at it, myself included. The human comedy.

Artists in the modern world certainly tend to hubris. Mann says somewhere a more modest position needs again to be found in which art is once again the servant of the community. But that place cannot be attained by giving up its role as rigorous conscience of the community and its duty of intellectual honesty. Mann writes dialectically in *Doctor Faustus*, "It is my conviction that mind, in its most audacious, unrestrained advance and researches, can, however unsuited to the masses, be certain in some indirect way to serve man—in the long run men." I remember Bahá'ís always wanted Shoghi Effendi to write on a simpler level for them. His response was that they should struggle to come up to his level. A hard counsel perhaps for many, but we see all around us now the kind of self-destructive society that results as the will weakens and much of which is the logical result of liberal thinking. It seems to me the general attitude of most Bahá'ís toward art also tends to go in the wrong direction.

Apparently we are moving to Parker, Arizona in August. I have many misgivings about it. The desert doesn't appeal to me at all. And it is really desert—dry, desiccated, nothing but rock, sand, mountains, cacti, and a few scrubby bushes. Where we will be living is an irrigated agricultural valley on the Colorado river, so it's a little better. I don't know. No other door out of here has opened, so we're going. It might be a good place to keep writing, no distractions, to say the least, if I can avoid depleting too much energy teaching.

I am worried I am going to have trouble getting books and magazines. I've been studying so long though, I have most of what I need and will learn to buy books more often through the mail, I suppose. I intend to subscribe to DIALOG. It's the best computer database in the world for serious research and will give me access to much information that I used to spend time running to the library to excavate. One can also order magazine articles and books directly through it. I hope it will compensate somewhat for the lack of a real library.

I tell myself it's time to start writing another book since I have certainly done enough background research for one over the last couple of years. The real barrier to writing it is the will to go on. I don't know anymore, perhaps I've failed and should withdraw into what one poet called a quiet obscurity, as though I have ever had anything else. Robert Frost says somewhere the poet can go on for only so long without some confirmation from the outside world. I've always felt an affinity with him, especially in terms of how long he had to wait. I'm afraid I have a rather stubborn streak in me. Either I've got it all wrong or there seems to be some kind of spiritual test in this for me. At times I wonder exactly what that might be and when, if ever, I'm going to pass it.

Pam will be teaching in a high school and I will be teaching in a community college. Probably a dead end and another waste of time. DEATH VALLEY! I am fending off memories of Augustine in the North African desert. I try to console myself with the thought that it's at least out on the periphery.

Once again I have to apologize for a letter that's much too long. I tried to keep it brief, but I guess I've mulled over many of these things for too many years to hold myself back from setting them down as fully and clearly as possible. I hope you realize I don't direct any of this at you personally. And I concede there are other points of view on these matters. For better or for worse, these are mine. I accept the consequences. At least until I'm persuaded by experience or argument to another view.

Your yard full of oak trees is very beautiful. I can well imagine that after a storm you would have quite a lot of branches to clean up. The Rochester I remember was the one of oak trees all along the roads, cows grazing on what's now Great Oaks, and very few apartments and condominiums—a place now of the imagination. Whenever I visit there I always grieve that the four and five lane highways have devoured so many trees. I am glad to hear you enjoy the ones you have.

Tahbo Road
Poston, Arizona

8 November 1990

Dear Elinor,

I apologize for taking so long to write to you from out here. At the time of my last letter we had not yet gotten the complete address of this house. I've been intending to write for weeks, but, as they say, it's been one thing after another.

At first I was preoccupied with rereading Gilbert Murray's book on the League and UN. Given the invasion of Kuwait, I studied it with perhaps more than my usual omnivorous attention to such matters. Then someone invited me to write an essay for a book on Saul Bellow, and, for more than a month, I have been reading everything by him from about the last thirty years. Actually, it occurs to me, Murray and Bellow share the recognition that liberalism has burned itself out and that something else is drastically needed. Murray never got too far with what that might be, nor has Bellow, though he has a very profound sense of the requirements of the human soul and a superb understanding of the spiritual crisis of modern civilization.

I have joked recently that living out here in the desert puts us on the collapsing edge of social breakdown. From a slightly different perspective, the problem is that civilization has yet to evolve out here. This is really a very isolated, backward area of the country. So much so, at times, I can't believe it. By and large, many of the Indians are in a very bad way, and many of the Hispanics have their own problems too. And then there is the pathetic plight of the whites, and the suburbanites from LA and elsewhere, like us. We're already hoping to get out of here as soon as possible.

I've been escaping via my computer modem which allows me

to connect with civilization several hundred miles away. DIALOG, the database I mentioned to you in my last letter, has turned out to be an incredible resource. I have been discovering what the "information age" is all about. To my amazement I have been reading accurately translated articles that are only a few months old from leading Russian literary journals in Moscow; browsing through articles from twelve major US newspapers, only one of which can be purchased within the surrounding 150 miles; using the best reference works that in the past required access to a university library; locating instantaneously every book in print by a particular author as well as a complete bibliography of published articles; ordering articles from the University of California at Berkeley with the touch of a few keys. All of this used to be an onerous chore. DIALOG is available from most countries in the world and with leading databases in literally every field of human endeavor—medicine, business, engineering, and so on. A quick look at their list of telephone numbers shows someone in Colombia, parts of Africa, or what used to be Kuwait could just as easily do what I am doing. Not long ago people didn't know the other side of the world even existed. Of course, one might add, there are many who still don't.

Another Air Force jet just went by. The military bases are a hundred to two hundred miles away but they zoom through here on their practice runs. On Monday I went out at about nine o'clock in the morning to put something in the mailbox. As I was walking the short twenty-five yards down the road I heard a jet at what I thought was some distance away. Suddenly I was shocked to see what looked like a F-16 fighter cruise past me at about twenty to thirty feet off the ground. It was less than a city block from me. Most other people probably wouldn't have been as affected by the sight as I was. It made me realize at a very deep emotional level what a highly militarized society we live in. As I recall living in Rochester and elsewhere, I never experienced such a thing. It's all kept much more distant, hidden away, out of mind. It made me think of a book by

Robert Nisbet, *The Present Age*, which criticizes the morally destructive influence of the military on modern life in America. Passages of the Guardian on the military build up of the 1930s, near the end of *The Advent of Divine Justice*, came to mind. I've been thinking too of Norman Angell's book *The Great Illusion*, written just before World War I. Its thesis is something like that in the modern world nothing can be gained from war between the nations because they have become too interdependent both economically and culturally. Though most of the jets are a little farther away than this particular one, several fly past each day. Last week there were three jets accompanying some kind of enormous bomber for some reason or another. I've noticed too that at night the bombers practice refueling out here. I assume it's practice.

It turns out that our immediate neighborhood, if it can be called that, was a concentration camp for Japanese-Americans. In the local Native-American museum there are pictures of the barracks that housed approximately five thousand people here, four and a half miles south of Poston, where we actually live. Parker is about twenty miles to the north. The only building still standing from that time is the old school building that was thrown up for the Japanese. Our house is about two blocks from it. In the museum there's a picture of a Kabuki play being performed on the school stage. I've never cared for Kabuki. It's too shallow for my tastes. I've always preferred the No plays and saw some excellent productions in Japan. It's what the playwright Zeami called *yugen* that appeals to me. It means something like the mystery and strangeness of life. Anyway, the same mountains are here but all that is gone. Just the mountains and the fields and one old building. But in some ways this was probably a good place to wait out the second world war.

It's usually very quiet here, and I can wake up at four or five and study or write. Although Pam expressed how we both feel at times when she grumbled recently she has suffered more from culture shock by moving out here than to Japan, we're doing fairly well.

It must be cold, perhaps even snowing, in Michigan by now. The temperature here was in the low to mid nineties throughout most of October. I hate the heat. The change of seasons is something I've always enjoyed very much. Here they say it's just one "beautiful" day after another all winter long. Elliot, though, hasn't suffered at all from his allergies this fall as he did during the last couple of years in Illinois. For that we're grateful. It was quite painful for him to cough uncontrollably for hours and extremely distressing for us to be unable to do anything to help him. I know you can understand this much more than most people. I hope the change of seasons hasn't affected your own condition adversely.

Your daughter Kathleen is telling you the right thing. Another twenty years! That's the way to think, no matter how much at times you might loathe the idea.

Poston, Arizona

10 April 1991

Dear Elinor,

How do I honestly answer your last letter? Already one feels a discrepancy has crept into one's spiritual life—one between what one feels and what has become acceptable utterance in limited Bahá'í circles. Truth has been relegated elsewhere. Or so it seems to me at times.

There's a passage in Dostoevsky's letters that I often think about. He mentions to a friend that he's a child of his century, a child of doubt and disbelief, who experiences in his soul agonizing antinomies between his thirst to believe and arguments against it. And you mention you take comfort that people in all religions have always struggled with their faith, with its unevenness and weakness. Robert Hayden and I used to discuss this kind of thing. He was a very deeply torn man. One, to whom, according to his own testimony, faith did not come easily, if at all. Saul Bellow talks somewhere of the "leprosy of souls." I fear I have picked up the disease from Hayden, if it wasn't in me to begin with. I am not sure, though, that it is a disease.

On the other hand, given the almost total emphasis on the administrative order, reasons abound for doubt. I share your Bob's distress over it. Shoghi Effendi warns somewhere that the administrative order should never become an end in itself, but I'm afraid that's exactly what has happened. It seems quite spiritually dead to me. All the cheap rhetoric about how "spiritual" administration really is can never hide that fact. There's a fine book by a Bahá'í, Peter Smith, in which he mentions quite rightly, I think, that metaphysics has become "relatively peripheral to central Bahá'í concerns." And there you have it. How similar to the society that surrounds us.

I met Mr. Khadem once at Bahá'í summer school in Michigan. I don't know if I'd use the word saintly, but he struck me as a very spiritually sensitive man, Hand of the Cause or not. There was somewhat of a trivial flap over whether Bahá'ís were improperly interpreting the *Hidden Words* and *The Seven Valleys*. He felt that they were and warned that stronger personalities (what a euphemism) would force their own interpretations on others. Everyone denied that that had ever happened. To me, though, that seemed to be exactly what had happened, and I said so. His acceptance of my carefully offered agreement was altogether unexpected. He warmly embraced me after the meeting ended with a "God bless you" that to me seemed all out of proportion to my little admission of common agreement. Strange to think of this incident after so many years, thirteen or so.

In studying the old religions I have always been struck by how early in their history the maladies that eventually undermined them first manifested themselves. Christianity and Islam are particularly good examples. Having a strong sense of history, I can't regard the Bahá'í Faith as any different. Indeed, the condition of the patient already seems terminal. In a naive way I would like to think otherwise, but honesty compels me to recognize it. That and repeated experience.

You mention the Universal House of Justice. I understand what you're saying about the human qualities of its members. I heard Glenford Mitchell speak at a conference and met him on another occasion long before he was elected. I was troubled by his statement to me, which I've always remembered: "It takes great creativity too to inspire people to action." There's something too Machiavellian in that for my tastes, not to mention insecure. One hopes the whole is more than the sum of its parts, but it is always difficult to see how that could be. Usually, in this world, individual defects are merely carried over into the whole. Instead of being mitigated, they can taint the entire organism. Such, to me, is human nature.

The leap of faith you talk about (Kierkegaardian, shall we

say?) is indeed a difficult one to make, especially since Shoghi Effendi specifically stated the UHJ has infallibility only in terms of legislation and not in interpretative matters, the power of which was solely to reside with the Guardian. With the death of Shoghi Effendi, the Faith has been, in a way, so it seems to me too, as you say, cast adrift. The leap of faith is rendered all the more difficult by what seems to me to be the attempt by the UHJ at times to fill the interpretative vacuum. I simply don't believe the individual members bring sufficient ability to the subtlety of some doctrinal issues, and it's reflected in their decisions or in their involvement in petty issues which really should be beneath their dignity. And then letters I've received from what passes for a Department of the Secretariat at the World Center have been an absolute joke. As a result of the illiteracy of a "secretary," I received one letter that was actually obscene. Rather hard to leap over such things. I'm afraid it's no better at the level of the NSA, here or in Japan. And then when it comes to the LSAs....

It seems to me that the fact some things were changed about the Guardianship raises serious questions. To say they can't be explained and must be accepted as is would appear to ignore how grave such cynical, deceitful acts are. I can understand your saying you believe this does not destroy the overall message. It is difficult not to think, though, that it calls into question the honesty and motivation of the people and institutions involved. "Overall" seems to allow that some damage has been done. Judging from some books that have appeared, I think intelligent people are well aware of such contradictions within the Faith. I can understand why such crackpot notions as telepathy, and so on, were dropped from earlier books, with no loss whatsoever, but it seems to have set a dangerous precedent and legitimized, perhaps, very cynical, pernicious attitudes among some in the administration of the Faith. Those attitudes will utterly destroy the Bahá'í Faith in the long run. At times the emphasis of some already seems to be largely on milking the masses of millions and keeping the enterprise going.

I've been reading Ibn Khaldun's *Introduction to History*, written in 1377, a work on the collapse of Berber Islamic society. I mentioned him to you some time ago. His work is often cited as the first sociological study of civilization. Though he breaks new ground, Khaldun draws in some respects on Plato's *Republic*. He was a Sunni Muslim and writes often of the corruption of the Sunni caliphate, after the first four caliphs, the only true ones to Khaldun, into royal authority. Looking back, I'm grateful I had a class on Islamic history at U of M with a Sunni Muslim from Cairo University because he dismissed Shiism as a schism. At one point Khaldun cites the tradition of Muhammad: "The caliphate after me will last thirty years; then, it will revert to being tyrannic royal authority." Unfortunately, some Persian Bahá'ís want to drag all the animosities between the Shí'ahs and Sunnis into the Bahá'í Faith. I could care less about all that and find it disillusioning that even the Guardian was not above carrying on the bigotries of Shí'ah Islam against the Sunnis and Westerners, when it served his purposes.

I suppose, as an American, I feel nothing but seething contempt for all those old world attitudes and can't conceive of belonging complacently to any religion that perpetuates them. For me, such attitudes, including those that surface in the Guardian's writings ("low-born Christian woman," "self-styled Vicar of the Prophet of God" PDC 98, etc.), are detritus from the past that deserve only to be swept away, though surely they played a useful role in motivating some Persian Bahá'ís. Despite the loss of the pristine state of Islam, Khaldun asserts, "There remained the traits that were characteristic of the caliphate, namely, preference for Islam and its ways, and adherence to the path of truth." (The "path of truth" is the Sunna or example of Muhammad.) Something like this has already occurred with the Bahá'í Faith. The lust for power or "royal authority" shows it, as Khaldun argues. To ignore it would be less than honest. Robert Hayden handled much of this well in his poem "The Night-Blooming Cereus":

Lunar presence,
foredoomed, already dying.

Khaldun makes a particularly Islamic observation at one point: "Political leadership, based either on religious or royal authority, is inevitable." Christianity often tried to evade or obscure this fact. The danger of such thinking, though, is that it can lead to Machiavellian deceit—in Khaldun's terms, to the lack of what is the primary requisite for cooperation and trust among men—restraint. The lack of ethics in the Marxist-Leninist ethos illustrates this well: The end justifies the means. I just don't see the Bahá'í Faith as yet sufficiently aware of the temptation of power or capable of resisting it.

When I think of what I have read about Quakers or Baptists, I remember their respect for the individual conscience or light. Historically, there was always the danger of that leading to antinomianism, but, at its best, such recognition of the validity of the individual's heeding the call of his own sincere conscience prevented many abuses that run rife through the history of more authoritarian religions, such as Catholicism. Ralph Waldo Emerson, of course, was often regarded as an antinomian by the early Unitarian church. His work represents a milestone on the development of modern individualism that has brought us as a society to the anarchy of today. And he certainly did much to depart from some of the tenets of Christianity as it progressively declined during the nineteenth century. Nietzsche thought Emerson prepared the way for modern nihilism, which I think is a misreading. But what else could Emerson have done? Placate a conventional Unitarianism? Dissent is not contention. Ultimately, Emerson stands vindicated before the tribunal of time that has proven he served the God who endowed him with a conscience and bade him to follow it, within the limitations imposed upon him. The religious history of Christianity shows dissent is something indispensable, in contrast to contention or dissension, and is necessary for religion itself to avoid becoming oppressive.

More than a year ago I corresponded briefly with a Bahá'í in Great Britain, named Geoffrey Nash. In 1984 he wrote a book on the Faith and modern cultural history, published by George Ronald. I had mentioned to him the possibility of starting a literary magazine. He commented on the experience of a little Bahá'í magazine, of very inferior quality, that's still, I believe, being published in California:

> We can see by what has happened to *Dialogue* that even if people are ready to read an independent style magazine, there are others who do not wish them to, and are prepared to make it virtually impossible for them to do so. Sorry to sound so bleak, but that is the reality of the situation.

I don't know all the details but it's a pity some apparently felt the need to enforce "unity." On the other hand, the first four issues of this magazine left me nauseated, and I dropped my subscription. The intellectual level was non-existent to pathetic, and the magazine was full of gullible, excessively liberal, and Marxist clichés. Even more vapid than *World Order*.

I've been quite disillusioned by the bellicose nationalism of the last few months. Very few observers have drawn the right lesson from the United Nation's involvement in the Gulf crisis. President Bush at times seems to understand quite well the wider implications but then falls short in important ways. And disorder seems to be increasing elsewhere. It is still possible Bush will make the right decisions when bitter experience leaves him no alternative. His time at the UN and the way he turned to it when he had to might be reasons for some small hope.

Somehow, slowly, gradually, painfully, God is bringing the nations together. Dag Hammarskjold wrote somewhere that he had little patience for theories and plans of how to accomplish it but rather preferred the periodic extension of UN authority as the result of experience and the response it necessitated from the world community. Though most still cling to nationalism, we have had a tremendous demonstration in the Gulf of the potential for world unity. Whatever future experience, the direction remains clear and an inescapable precedent has been set, one that can be further built on, or on its ashes. Yet I find it difficult to put any credence in what has been called a "new world order." So far, it seems to be just more of the old one.

Another outpouring, I'm afraid. You must think, "What did I do to deserve this?" You might recall you and Bob put in Rochester's library that old copy of *Bahá'u'lláh and the New Era*, the one I stumbled onto many years ago. I hold no grudge.

We've had Michigan summer weather here now for a couple of months. We are warned that soon the Arizona summer will begin. We're not sure we're ready, but there's no avoiding it.

I hope you are finding peace of mind and happiness. And some relief from your allergies. Rare treasures in this world.

Poston, Arizona

4 May 1992

Dear Elinor,

Thank you for your kind letter. Don't worry about taking so long to write. We're operating under no pressure here.

Kierkegaard's leap of faith, of course, had to do with belief in God. I've never had any great agony in that regard. I've always had at least some degree of intuitive certainty in the existence of—well, use any traditional word you want, God, I suppose. For Kierkegaard, as for most existential philosophers, belief was absurd, an act of desperation. In order to live in the modern world, one had to "leap . . . into the arms of God." Tertullian had essentially said the same thing about Christianity in ancient Rome: "It is certain because it is impossible." In contrast to both, Abdul-Baha states faith is "conscious knowledge." Similarly, Thomas Aquinas, no angst in him, had believed that faith is a type of knowledge. To shift the problem of faith to epistemology is an idea that fascinates me, though Abdul-Baha also says somewhere that only when one knows in the heart will one believe.

The leap you talk about, however, is different from Kierkegaard's and not as simple as it is made out to be. Shoghi Effendi writes somewhere that the administrators of Bahá'u'lláh must be worthy of the trust of the Bahá'í community. Undeniable experience has shown me that is not always the case. It seems to me the Bahá'í administration, or what passes for it, is well on its way to becoming its own form of clergy, with all the abuses and seductions of the past. The worst distortions of the Jesuits or mullahs seem suggestive. If God has given us a mind to use, I don't see how ignoring or lying about the situation serves any purpose, except the acquisition of further power and control.

The Bahá'í Faith has become very oppressive and manipulative of the individual. That to me is merely a statement of fact, as I have experienced it, for nearly sixteen years now. The usual stratagem in dealing with anyone who would express his conscience in good faith is to pretend the Cause is above any kind of criticism whatsoever while intimating that anyone who would speak honestly must have something wrong with him, i.e., his spiritual life isn't what it should be, he doesn't understand the nature of unity, or he's accused of trying to obtain power for himself, which at times seems merely a calculated way of discrediting the person, and so on. Another common strategy used to acquire control over the individual is to humor the person by letting him pour himself out, etc., and then self-righteously giving him the Truth.

All this was brought home to me again by our experience at the Seventh Annual Bahá'í Grand Canyon Conference in Phoenix last year at the end of December. Basically, it was an Iranian social at the Hyatt. I had an interesting discussion with a Bahá'í from Los Angeles, married to a Persian, about the gross incompetence of the assembly there, which, you might recall, the NSA disbanded some years ago.[1] After discussing for some time the pronounced ignorance of the average Persian for the political and cultural history of the Western world, including the United States, he stated the new assembly really isn't any better. As he put it, the Persians more or less run the show for themselves while everyone else just goes along with it. Apathy was a word he also used.

One afternoon as we were waiting for the elevator to take us down for lunch, a lovely little Persian girl, about eleven or so, bounced up with a friend and pushed the button while saying, "Okay, but we'll have to wait for the old man." To me it

---

[1]Juan R. I. Cole. "Race, Immorality and Money in the American Baha'i Community: Impeaching the Los Angeles Spiritual Assembly." *Religion* 30, 2 (2000): 109-125.

typified the spirituality so many Persians inculcate in their children, the example they set, while blabbering about the decadence of America.

Before we were married, Pamela had a fairly close relationship with a South-American Persian Bahá'í at Hope College. He usually refused to talk to her about the Bahá'í Faith. He was the son of a "prominent" Bahá'í, a counselor, member of sundry international Bahá'í boards, advice-giver to the UHJ, one of the holy Afnáns, I believe. Their relationship eventually fell apart for good reasons but not before exposing her to the high morals actually in effect among some Persian Bahá'ís. It's a wonder she ever became a Bahá'í. Following the demise of their relationship, the son had an affair with a married woman, a Bahá'í, whom he and the father regarded somewhat as, to use the unflattering Jewish term, a shiksa. The exploitation was that calculating and base, and the father knew about it. It's best to leave a lot unsaid. Still, his calling Pam a week after his marrying someone else and claiming he still cared for her so much, etc., came as a shock. That was, of course, after she had been married to me for some time. His most recent attempt to call Pam was last year. We occasionally read about his and his family's selfless service to the Faith. At one conference session I attended, a member of the NSA pointed out that only about 680 people entered the Faith during the last year in the US. As he put it, that really isn't very good. That's usually, though, what it's been for a very long time. I was not surprised to hear so few people entered the Faith and doubt anyone in the audience was. What surprises me is that some apparently can't understand why the "troops" aren't pouring in.

You mention Louhelen's experiment with a college program failing. It seems to me it was doomed from the beginning. At the time when it was first announced I was struck by the shamelessly cynical use of inner city and rural youth, as though their lives amounted to so little the Faith was justified in experimenting on them. How instructive that the doors were not knocked down by Persian and white Bahá'ís from the suburbs trying to get their children in. If anyone in the Faith had actually cared about doing those young people some good in the first place, they would have directed them to a decently established college instead of exploiting their idealism and trust. I don't harbor any great hope for Louhelen becoming an illustrious Bahá'í university. Last year I noticed somewhere, in response to a statement of the UHJ, an announcement for a meeting at Louhelen to discuss what could be done to bring in more "people of capacity." Participants were urged to bring their favorite board game to play afterwards. That's the kind of low-level affair at which the Bahá'í Faith excels.

For the first time since the Robert Hayden Fellowship was begun at Louhelen in 1985, I sent in March a SASE for information on it. That was more than seven weeks ago, five before their deadline of the 21st of April. No surprise. Years ago Erma Hayden had mentioned to me they were instituting the Fellowship. I recall saying to her, "Oh, my, I can just imagine what that's going to amount to."

For some reason the banality of Louhelen makes me think of a memorial dinner held in Ann Arbor after Robert Hayden's funeral. Several professors from U of M and elsewhere attended. One of them said to me, "The Bahá'ís don't understand what they've got in Robert Hayden." At the time it had already seemed to me to be very much the case. Bob had said to me once, to my consternation, that I was the only Bahá'í who had ever really taken an interest in his work. More than a decade later I'm still appalled at the lack of understanding among Bahá'ís of what he managed to accomplish, alone, unaided, and held in contempt for the most part.

I appreciate your sending me the pieces on the early days of the Faith. The one on Tagore and the Unitarian Church was especially interesting to me. Many years ago I bought an old original edition of his *Gitanjali*, which I still have, and read other things by him. With time and further study, though, I found the later Tagore more fascinating and instructive—the one who, in the thirties, turned somewhat to communism, went to the USSR, and, after being shown a Potemkin village, failed to have the spiritual resources to see it for what it was. All that vague, attenuated spirituality amounting to so little in the end. Similarly, most of the Protestant denominations have diluted the reality of evil. The articles made me think too of what one Bahá'í has written somewhere or another on the early days of the Faith, how it really grew out of a kind of "cultic milieu." Fine phrase. Shoghi Effendi, coming out of Oxford, saw it for what it was. So he summed up *The Star of the West*, typical of that whole mind-set, in his last letter, if memory serves, to appear in it, as "insignificant." Surely, most Bahá'ís at the time failed to comprehend that. Increasingly, it seems to me Bahá'ís need to let go of the Persian propensity for oriental despotism and the American cultic milieu. To do that, there's got to be freedom to think and test and probe what it means to be a Bahá'í in the modern world. Exactly what's sadly lacking. The administration, in its infinite wisdom, its attempt to fill the interpretative void, has it all figured out—and woe unto him who would dare say otherwise.

You may find it very hard to understand why I choose not to sweep all this under the rug, in the name of so-called unity—a word that at times appears to have a euphemistic ring to it and may be basically a fraud, the result of oppressive tactics used to stifle all real thought and discussion in order to maintain a Machiavellian grasp on the reins of power. I am not one who can ignore the immense abyss between ideal and reality. And I don't believe it's right to lie, cheat, and deceive for the Bahá'í Faith.

If all the administration is going to amount to is another deceitful method for the exploitation of the masses, the world is much better off without it.

I identify somewhat with Ibn Khaldun: Paradoxically, now that I'm convinced the Faith has been hamstrung, I can give it my wholehearted support.

I've been reading lately a narrative poem by Robert Browning, "Bishop Blougram's Apology." I've read it a number of times over the years, and it's one that I continue to think about. The character of the bishop is partly based on John Henry Newman and another contemporary figure in the Roman Catholic Church, the latter of whom was especially noted for his abuse of power and position. Over dinner, the bishop justifies his corruption to a young journalist who has noticed his calculation, insincerity, and hypocrisy. In much of the poem, Browning is dealing with the nature of religious doubt. While the bishop is a hypocrite who embraces Catholicism because it gives him "cabin comforts" and the "estimation" of the masses, the journalist is charmingly naive in his insistence that religious faith should be "absolute." In a marvelous passage Browning recognizes the complex duality of the human soul:

> No, when the fight begins within himself,
> A man's worth something. God stoops o'er his head,
> Satan looks up between his feet—both tug—
> He's left, himself, i' the middle: the soul wakes
> And grows. Prolong that battle through his life!
> Never leave growing till the life to come! ll. 690

Putting this truth in a sophist's mouth, Browning probes much deeper into the struggle for faith than the "pious" usually allow themselves. To my mind, the health of the spirit requires that freedom—given by God—to doubt and question and probe every single dogma of religion in its oppressively organized phase. On the other hand, Browning's point is partly that doubt itself, like evil and suffering, is a test of one's belief, for mature belief can only grow out of the struggle with doubt.

There is something deeply, inescapably, eternally dialectical in the human being and in the very nature of existence, the way it develops, evolves, progresses.

Dostoevsky, in his chapter "The Grand Inquisitor," in *The Brothers Karamazov*, meditates dialectically on the dilemma of free will and obedience to religious authority. Christ returns during the Spanish Inquisition and is imprisoned by the Grand

Inquisitor who accuses Christ of leading men into confusion by giving them freedom of choice and conscience. The Grand Inquisitor informs Christ that "We have corrected Your work and have now founded it on miracle, mystery, and authority. And men rejoice at being led like cattle again, with the terrible gift of freedom that brought them so much suffering removed from them."

The Inquisitor goes on to tell Christ that man's "greatest need on earth" is "to find someone to worship, someone who can relieve him of the burden of his conscience, thus enabling him finally to unite into a harmonious ant-hill where there are no dissenting voices. . . ." In place of individual responsibility to God, the Inquisitor promises to free mankind from "the frightening torment they know today when they have to decide for themselves how to act." Christ listens to this sophist without uttering a word, and then, at the end, before being allowed to leave, rises and kisses the Inquisitor. Ivan, a nihilist, who relates this story, asserts all too accurately that in the modern world "everything is permitted." The Grand Inquisitor, grasping for power, a character to whom Nietzsche must have responded deeply, "doesn't believe in God." Dostoevsky knew these rich tensions were part of human nature. At times, the Bahá'í administration grossly fails to understand that Bahá'u'lláh has also blessed humankind with this burden of freedom and responsibility.

I've been reading St. Augustine's *City of God* for the past few months. I've always wanted to read it after having studied the Late Roman Empire and having read his *Confessions* a number of times. Since reading Rousseau's *Confessions* last year, I've also been wanting to go deeper into Augustine. His work is so different from the modern world and the problems that began, to some extent, with Rousseau. Actually, I've been rereading too Plato's *Republic* and Ibn Khaldun's *Muqaddimah* (Introduction). I've been deeply moved at how these great works ponder so many of the same problems of religious belief and true civilization. You may laugh, but, during the last few days, I've been ploughing through *The Federalist* too, another book I've felt for years compelled to read. Coming after some of the above reading, I've relished its very different approach to human meaning and organization and have been struck by how reminiscent the current chaos in the former Soviet Union is to our own woes under the Articles of Confederation. Saul Bellow remarked in an interview once that in the modern democracies a contract was offered to the majority and plainly spelled out in *The Federalist*: "We will provide for your real needs. You will be fed and protected, you will live in peace. As for the life of the imagination, unfortunately we can't do much for you in that respect. Scientific imagination, yes. That must and will thrive, but as for esthetic imagination—forget it."

Though I respect immensely the political system the federalist papers helped create, there is a sense in which Bellow's evocative reading is suggestive. The Framers were quite conscious that the new political order relegated the spiritual and the imagination to the sidelines. Yet they produced a system, at its best, that allowed diversity and tolerance a little more room to develop. Unfortunately, as it has devolved, indifference or hostility often predominate, with chaos and anomie running close behind. At least, though, it is, as Shoghi Effendi called it, "an immortal System," one that somewhat works, which is all the Founders ever claimed for it. Alexander Hamilton memorably phrased it: "I never expect to see a perfect work from imperfect man." What we see now, all around us, is the failure of most of what the Enlightenment produced, both communism and secular liberal democracy. Though based on the same secular principles too, the UN is the obvious immediate heir to the best in the political tradition of world civilization.

Bellow is referring, though, to the role of the spiritual under such a political regime and the concomitant contempt for the arts as mere entertainment and fluff, which they often are, in their debased form. Similarly, in an interview, Robert Hayden said once, "since the arts do involve the spiritual and do involve spiritual vision, there is not much concern with that." This loss of respect for the role the spiritual plays in the arts has been one of the scourges of modern society. It's symbolic of the spiritual vacuum, the malaise of modern society. Having shut itself off to spiritual values—which only religion truly gives and the creative imagination is capable of productively meditating on—modern society continues to deteriorate for lack of them. Such artists as Thomas Mann understood quite well what modern bourgeois materialism meant in spiritual terms. As a result he and other artists had, what a literary critic named Lionel Trilling perceptively called, "the adversary intention" toward modern civilization. Not pretending themselves capable of revealing a new religion and unable to deny the increasing social corruption that resulted from the lack of spiritual values, modern artists chose to try to shock people into the recognition that there is an abyss under their feet, an abyss the average person seeks to ignore though the situation continues to worsen.

Because society itself is involved in this conundrum, artists cannot resolve it alone. Trilling mentions the usual position of artists throughout history has been support of prevailing social values. With the loss of religious belief and consensus that role has inevitably changed and mutual recognition and support have disappeared. And with the corruption of social values, what the prevailing society holds sacred has been transmogrified into pervasive turpitude, which the best artists refuse to embrace, while most of the less gifted spread the disease. How society and artists can find a way back toward agreement remains a true dilemma. Most Bahá'ís like to think simplistically that the Faith has the answer, but, it seems to me, most Bahá'í administrators are just as philistine as the surrounding society. Like administrators under communism, or democracy for that matter, they regard the arts as cheap fluff whose role is merely to put icing on the cake and prop them up. Art does enculturate values, largely as spin off, but it does much more than that. And, it also seems to me, the worst of the unsophisticated in the administration ridiculously assume writers should be Bahá'í versions of Rumi or Hafez. All that has been done, though, as they say. Artists have to work with where the arts and society are today, not five-hundred years ago. One would think such a thing would be self-evident. The very notion of building bridges presupposes touching something like land on each side. If the history of the arts shows anything, it's that the unimaginative are seldom happy with the vision of serious art.

Shoghi Effendi states somewhere to the effect that when literature begins to give expression to the message of the Faith that is when real growth will take place. There are many historical parallels that suggest this may be the case. It seems to me, though, that, for this to happen, there are numerous prerequisites that have yet to be met. The best artists are not going to support an administration that doesn't demonstrate it is indeed worthy of support. The inevitable question one must ask oneself is whether the administration is fit to bear the power one's art is helping it acquire. Robert Hayden, in this sense, may prove instructive. He suggested to me more than once that he had given too much, too easily, to an incompetent administration that didn't sufficiently realize what it had in fact been given. Mistaking art for propaganda, some have largely dismissed, or missed, the entire cultural context of his work and trivialized the profundity of it.

Bahá'u'lláh talks somewhere about to each their own. This is an idea that is expressed in all the great religions. Augustine mentions in *The City of God* the "mutual recognition of rights" makes a mob into a people. One of the destructive aspects of democracy is that it confuses society by claiming all people are equal, not merely before God or the law, but within the social order, which of necessity must be hierarchical. It seems to me the administration is all-too-quick to sermonize about what is owed by the people to it and woefully slow to recognize what it owes to them. Reciprocity has often been construed as the foundation of civilization. I remember Confucius thought of it as such.

I've been studying Latin for about three months and have

made fairly good progress. I'm hoping to read the Roman epic poet Virgil in the original or at least some of the most important passages of his *Aeneid*. At times I think of returning to the Catholic church. It at least remembers Jesus cared for the poor and actually puts its money where its mouth is, more than any other organization, and often has. I've discovered too that there are intelligent Catholics who understand some of my work quite well. Recently, the editor of a largely Catholic magazine I've published in wrote me a letter of recommendation in which he says my work "constitutes a diligent and honest search for general principles of order, without which a civilization perishes." He surprised me when he compared my perspective to "Emerson's famous phrase, 'man thinking'" and among Irving Babbitt's "keen-sighted few." Not the kind of thing an Oxford Ph.D. and Fellow of the Royal Society for the Arts writes indiscriminately. I don't know.... It depresses me, really. Of course, he doesn't know I'm a Bahá'í, or I assume he doesn't. The fact that I am is out there, and I've never gone out of my way to conceal it, nor to wear it on my shirt sleeve in some cheap, fanatical, and flashy way, which seems what the average Bahá'í thinks artists ought to do and which a shallow administration encourages. He's read most of my essays, which I have always thought were following Kierkegaard in some respects and Rilke's aphorism, from Rodin, "patience, always patience," by using universal terms without crude proselytizing. Unlike the Marxists, formalists, and other charlatans in the humanities these days, he at least understands and respects the spiritual and moral impetus behind my writing—much better than the average illiterate Bahá'í or American. Given my seemingly endless experience with how utterly inept *World Order* is, the only show in town, pathetic as it is—I find it difficult not to consider during weak moments going backwards. The only thing that prevents me is "I am the way, the truth, and the life." That's a stumbling block I leapt over a long, long time ago. I have savored too much the truth of other religions and its reflection in literature. I believe in the revelation of Bahá'u'lláh.

It's the oppression of the administration that fills me with disgust, and its penchant for tawdry, soul-stifling, bourgeois slop instead of art.

Have you had a chance to read Edith Hamilton's *The Greek Way*? I reread it last August as background for a class I was scheduled to teach down here on Homer and Greek drama. To no surprise, the class didn't make the necessary enrollment, but I enjoyed looking at it again. She has a very profound understanding of the intimate connection between tragedy and the spiritual. Some years ago I published an essay on Sophocles and found her reading of his plays unusually perceptive. I especially respond to her comments on Sophocles and Milton.

Have you been following the development of the UN since the Security Council summit in January? The summit declaration itself is a remarkable document that may bode very well indeed for the future. In addition now to the various efforts at peacemaking, it is the first hard, inescapable evidence to my skeptical mind that the "new world order," the secular one, is beginning to take concrete form. Despite the fact that what used to be the Soviet Union remains highly unstable, there may now be more reason for hope than has existed for a very long time. And regardless of resurging nationalism, here and abroad, very great changes at the UN have already taken place—the magnitude of which it seems most people simply don't have the foggiest notion.

I don't suppose much more will happen until after the election this fall. Yet who knows. The process has clearly taken on a new momentum of its own. Given what's already taken place, the right concatenation of events might push for very rapid change. Such things always make me worry, though. I'm hoping for the slow but continual unfolding of the principles of the UN Charter and the broadening of its scope, as the January summit meeting envisioned.

At the back of my mind I still fear those words of Shoghi Effendi from 1957 in *Messages to the Bahá'í World*:

> . . .the retributive calamity which, as decreed by Him Who is the Judge and Redeemer of mankind, must, sooner or later, afflict a society which, for the most part, and for over a century, has turned a deaf ear to the Voice of God's Messenger in this day. . . . (MBW 103)

Frail human being that I am, I'm now hoping that those words too prove to be excessive rhetoric, probably destined to be quietly deleted from some future edition or reinterpreted away as metaphorically fulfilled.

The weather is as boring as usual out here. How we long for a torrential Michigan thunderstorm! And the snow you describe would be manna from heaven! Instead, the sweltering heat is beginning. Along with the dust storms. Correction. Those can happen year round. T. S. Eliot's words from *The Waste Land* have come to mean much more to me:

> Here is no water but only rock
> Rock and no water and the sandy road
> The road winding above among the mountains
> Which are mountains of rock without water
> If there were water we should stop and drink . . .

Lately it's been going up over 105 degrees, but no humidity, dry as a bone.

Sorry to hear about your mishap sliding into a snowbank. That is certainly one thing about Michigan and Illinois we don't miss! Glad it turned out all right for you. I'm sure you must have been shaken up, though.

We're considering moving to Lake Havasu City. On the positive side, it's at least, on the surface, definitely post-Christian, postmodern late twentieth-century America though it too lacks a decent library. There's a Bahá'í who's lived there for twenty-one years with whom we celebrated Naw Ruz this year.

A few months ago, I wrote a poem on the Japanese

internment camp here on the reservation. I've been joking with Pam that I'm now ready and eager to move on. Actually, living out here has truly helped me to understand much more how thoroughly bankrupt modern society is. An Indian reservation is a marvelous place from which to view the works of the Enlightenment. And any vague liberal sentimentality I might have had about Native-Americans has been thoroughly lessoned. I am grateful that we've met some people who are quite vocal about their own antipathy to the exploitation of Indians by radicals of various stripes.

I hope you are enjoying some relief from your chemical sensitivities. Am I wrong to think there are periods when they're a little easier to endure? Elliot has had more trouble this spring than last with the desert pollens or whatever. Some people move out here expecting to escape their allergies but actually end up worse off. He hasn't reached that stage though friends claim he probably will. Pam has been having trouble lately with some kind of reaction to something out here too.

Oh no, I fear, another horribly long letter....

As always, best wishes,

Fred

Godfrey Road
Godfrey, Illinois

23 February 1994

Dear Elinor,

I'm sorry for not having written sooner. I can't believe it's going on two years since I wrote you last, and we've been back here in Illinois for more than a year and a half.

I hope your health is holding out for you and even giving you a rest, here and there.

The move back to Illinois from Arizona just dropped out of nowhere at the end of the summer back then, in 1992, and I've been rather overwhelmed with tedious duties and the struggle to keep any real work going forward. In some ways, though, finding this job teaching non-Western literature has been fortunate. It first took a year to develop the course and get it approved by the state college board. During that time I was able to teach some classes that have been very useful at least to my own development. I began with a humanities survey of Western civilization from Sumer to the late Roman Empire, taught a number of classes of American literature from the Puritans to the twentieth century, and also taught World literature in which I focussed on epic poetry from the Greeks to Milton. After my studies in the desert, I came to realize I could use these courses to consolidate my gains, such as they were.

This semester is just about the first one in which I've taught the same class twice, non-Western literature, so I'm under a little less pressure finally. I have found teaching non-Western literature challenging and stimulating. The class covers India, China, Japan, Africa, and the Middle East—a very broad survey, to say the least, which suits me fine. Though I had several relevant courses at U of M, I've always read a lot of literature from other parts of the world. Teaching this course has given me the time to study at an even deeper level works that I had read on my own long ago as well as new pieces I had never gotten around to reading. Since I've been here I've also attended four conferences on East Asia with University of Chicago faculty who opened up for me at least some new perspectives, though at times I've been very disappointed at how little some of them know about Japan and its literature.

It's kind of you to share with me the letter from Bob W. By and large, his struggles, though, aren't really mine either. I grew up vaguely a Catholic of sorts and have some understanding for the evil necessity of an institutional organization, though basically nothing but contempt for the Church's power-mongering. He seems to me to idealize primitive cultures all too much. In fact, he makes me think of Rousseau's idealization of the "noble savage" in the pristine state of "Nature." His description of forest people in Malaysia also reminds me of Margaret Mead's tendentious book *Coming of Age in Samoa*, one of Rousseau's modern progeny.

Elinor, you say, "I fear your hopes for the Baha's (sic) are beyond anything we can expect to see in our lifetimes." There is a sense in which your saying this to me is instructive. I have never in my heart of hearts felt I expected anything of Bahais. Indeed, with every passing year, I fear my expectations are diminishing. Remember, I came to the Faith through reading the Writings on my own. But you help me to realize that the fervor of my loathing is in itself a type of hope, misplaced. Perhaps there is a level of sober maturity there I need to strive for.

Thank you for the book by Marzieh Gail. Years ago I looked at it a little and thought little of it even way back then. It's very simplistic in approach and suffused with the Philistinism and anti-intellectualism that are so typical of most of the Persian Baha'is I've ever met.

Someone from the Alton Baha'i community called this evening. She wanted to ask Elliot if he knew where a book was that had been used a few weeks ago in his Baha'i class. Nobody could find it for this week. Of course he didn't have the foggiest idea. Some months ago a different Alton Baha'i was telling me that he was helping to install surveillance cameras in the National Center in Wilmette because office workers have been stealing from the contributions to the Fund. I have heard over in St. Louis the Baha'i community lost ten thousand dollars they had saved up for a down payment on a Baha'i center. The LSA's treasurer absconded with it all.

I once met a Persian administrator who said to me, "It's too early for what you're trying to do." Have I told you this before? I was too young and awed by his "prominence" to have the presence of mind to point out that God has given me life, I'm here today, called, so it seems to me, to fulfill my own individual destiny.

I've enclosed a Statement of Plans I put together last fall for a writer's grant. I doubt anymore such things will ever come through for me. After watching and applying to many councils for the humanities, etc., during the last several years, I've come to believe most of them are more interested in funding, well, I hesitate to say it, but surely you've read it at times, things like photographs of anal intercourse and homosexuality, and so on. Such things make me wonder if the olden times of individual patronage didn't work better than all the publicly and corporately funded institutions the arts have today that often seem to me to be merely perpetuating the status quo—and we know what that is. Someone like the Countess of Pembroke or Can Grande Della Scala did more for literature and for cultivating a civilized order than all the modern, egalitarian hype about funding the arts today would have us believe.

I've recently been struck by the idea that I should include the Shrine of the Báb in some way in the religious sites mentioned. I've been making notes on this poem for many years. At times I still despair I'll ever be able to write it. I've always been very conscious that the best epic poets of the past took several years to a decade to write their poems. In one way or another, they were able to find the necessary time and, in most cases, sufficient peace of mind to work uninterrupted, or in spite of it all. I fear that may all be beyond me now.

During the last month I've received two pieces of unexpected news: one, a Fulbright-Hays grant to China has gone through; two, I've been denied tenure, such as it is, at this mediocre community college. The denial of tenure also resulted in what would have been a loan on our first house falling through. I haven't told my family about the loss of the job, since it's all still in dispute, or the real reason the house fell through, and they would only be alarmed anyway. Most of my colleagues support me and are putting together a petition (28 have signed it!) calling on the Board of Trustees to reconsider and rescind the decision of the particular administrator involved. It's all very political and distressing and I'll spare you all the dreary details. Part of the situation, though, involves people in the English Department who are actuated by religious and racial discrimination. I wrote a short summary of events for the Illinois Education Association (union for community colleges) and have enclosed a copy thinking you might find it interesting. A few local Bahai zealots are part of the problem.

Oddly enough, I will apparently still be going to China. Although I'm very worried at this stage that the particular administrator may try to nix it, the Fulbright-Hays ought to be beyond her reach. Unfortunately, I'll have to take on the institutional part of the funding, five hundred dollars, and then an additional thousand or more because the Department of Education was able to underwrite only about ninety percent of the proposal. Nevertheless, we've decided it's something I ought to do, considered from every angle. Not only will it help me understand more about China for my writing, but also it ought to help me find, sooner or later, a job somewhere else. Of course I'm hoping that in the long run I'll end up someplace more conducive to my writing though that's purely speculative at this point. In the meantime, I'm doing everything possible to attempt to hold on to this job. For various reasons, I've often thought this job would only last for about two years but never expected it would be at someone else's choosing.

If China does come through, briefly, I'd spend three weeks in Beijing and take several seminars at Beijing University. After seeing the Peking opera, the Wall, the Forbidden City, etc., we'd go on to X'ian, the location of the huge discovery of ancient terra cotta soldiers and other historical temples and landmarks. From there, it would be the Buddhist caves of Dunhuang, out in the northern Gobi desert, on the old silk road. A long flight, then, across China to Guangzhou, near Hong Kong, a seminar or two at the major university of the area, and so forth. After some time in Hong Kong, we'll fly to Taiwan for about a week of seminars at the Academia Sinica in Taipei, among other venues. Five weeks in all. I'm leaving a lot out, but it still sounds too good to be true.

It has all hit Pamela harder than me. I've been through a lot of struggle during my life and am fairly tough. I'm afraid all the years of hardship are catching up more with her. She had hoped we could finally settle down and live a normal life. We've been married fourteen years, and this has been our first taste of that. I worry too about Elliot and Ethan not having the stability and deep friendships they need. All I can do now is apply for everything and hope for the best. And trust in God, "He Who holdeth the keys and unlocketh the doors."

I'm sorry to have such a mixture of good and ill to report. I hope you don't feel burdened by any of it. I don't intend that. Like most writers, I desire to write the cipher of my soul as honestly as I can. The equation would be incomplete were I to leave out the dualism that is life.

When I began this letter I had sworn to myself for your sake that I wasn't going to allow it to turn into a ten-pager. With the addenda, if I don't end now, I'll surely break that promise.

I hope you got your wordprocessor and are getting the hang of it and enjoying it.

Yours, as ever, Fred

Statement of Plans

For more than a decade I have been studying for and planning to write a serious epic poem titled "The Parliament of Poets."

I derive this title from both Chaucer and Attar, which suggests my focus is both Western and non-Western human experience. I seek to sift, ponder, and sum up not only American historical experience but the human experience of the major regions of the globe under the impact of modernism.

The Argument: The Guide takes the Persona on a Journey to meet all the great poets of the nations and to call them to assemble on the moon to debate the meaning of modern nihilism. All the great shades appear at the Apollo landing site in the Sea of Tranquillity: Homer and Virgil from our Greek and Roman foundation; Dante, Spenser, and Milton hail from the Judeo-Christian West; Rumi, Attar, and Hafez step forward from Islam; Tu Fu and Li Po, Basho and Zeami, step forth from China and Japan; the poets of the Bhagavad Gita and the Ramayana meet on that plain; griots from Africa; shamans from Indonesia and Australia; poets and seers of all ages, bards and minstrels, ancient and modern, major and minor, hail across the halls of time and space. As the Guides show the Persona crucial sites around the globe, such as Chartres Cathedral and the temples of Nara and Kyoto, the nature of social order and civilization in the regions of the past is explored. Modern twentieth century historical experience in all its glory and all its brutal suffering is fully confronted. The modern movement toward a global civilization is recognized and celebrated for the unprecedented future it opens to human beings. That transcendent rose symbol of our age, the Earth itself viewed from the heavens, one world with no visible boundaries, metaphor of the oneness of the human race, reflects its blue-green light into the darkness of the starry universe.

Undergirding my writing is my belief in the gradual,

continuing development of international federal institutions. The whole situation with the collapse of communism and with the numerous regional crises since then demonstrates that the slowly, painfully evolving authority of the United Nations remains the only hope for a comparatively peaceful world.

During the last several years I have read well over two hundred books on the League and the United Nations. For the most part they are dry technical manuals or histories of primary use to diplomats and scholars. Conversely, through the actions of concrete characters, epic poems interpret history. Global social conditions have more than sufficiently changed to warrant a fundamental reevaluation of what has become prevailing literary thinking.

As a member of the Baha'i Faith, I share its tragic vision of the unity of all religions and the oneness of humankind.

Signposts of a Journey

A Vision

Antinomies... 1996 - 2000

One of William Butler Yeats's Frustrators came to me in the night and recited, "All the gains of man come from conflict with the opposite of his true being. Has not Baha'u'llah taught you this?"

Upon waking, I was somewhat disturbed by this revelation and rummaged around my study for my copy of *A Vision*, whereupon I read, "Dante suffering injustice and the loss of Beatrice, found divine justice and the heavenly Beatrice."

Like Yeats, a Vision of "metaphors for poetry," "a last act of defence against the chaos of the world."

* * *

Antinomy is presupposed. There is tragedy in Baha'u'llah's writings, tragedy Baha'is like you typically fail to understand.

* * *

The lack of complexity is what concerns me, and the lack of acknowledgment of proportion.

* * *

It has never truly healed the patient. Baha'u'llah, unlike Baha'is, understands the condition is terminal....

* * *

Ecclesiastes perceived it long ago: "The heart of the sons of men is full of evil." Similarly, in "Young Goodman Brown," Hawthorne wrote, "Evil is the Nature of Mankind."

In *Some Answered Questions*, Abdul-Baha says evil "continues and endures." Not at all an upbeat modern concept full of psychological hope, delusion really....

* * *

"Alas, there is no Eden without its Serpent."
—Robert Hayden

* * *

"I have sworn eternal hostility to all forms of Tyranny against the minds of man." —Thomas Jefferson

* * *

You make me think of James Madison in the *Federalist Papers*: "I never expect to see a perfect thing from imperfect man." An exceedingly Western, Christian, American notion, though all the great religions have a sense of the limitations and modest possibilities of the human material, which such cultures as Iran blithely ignore in their futile search for perfection and obedience.

* * *

Twenty years of experiencing it.... and the sincere desire to see the faith reach the masses.... I don't believe it ever will if individuals continue throttling all genuinely held religious conscience and belief. Baha'u'llah understood the antinomies in the human soul.... that they're grounded in the free will god has given the human creature....

* * *

I believe so too. Shallow minds, though, can't see it, let alone begin to understand the antinomies Baha'u'llah knew God had kneaded into the human soul....

* * *

That's the way I see it.... Only Philistinism is welcomed in this religion—not the rich tensions of what is truly worthy of the name of art.... Rich tensions grounded in the antinomies of the human heart....

* * *

Only in public.... What many Baha'is claim Baha'u'llah "says" on this or that is merely what they themselves believe he says.... Or it is what a Shiite Bahai interpreter has told them Baha'u'llah "says." Baha'u'llah's own writings embrace powerful human antinomies, rich in the tension of lived life, not theoretical idealism, if you will.... True art probes those realities of life and the soul, trusting in God's creation; kitsch repeats a script.

* * *

"...indicative of both the light of reunion and the fire of separation." —Baha'u'llah

* * *

"This thing of darkness I acknowledge mine."
—Prospero

* * *

I recall John Milton's great words from *Areopagitica*: "I cannot praise a fugitive and cloistered virtue, unexercised and unbreathed, that never sallies out and sees her adversary, but slinks out of the race where that immortal garland is to be run for, not without dust and heat. Assuredly we bring not innocence into the world, we bring impurity much rather: that which purifies us is trial, and trial is by what is contrary. That virtue therefore which is but a youngling in the contemplation of evil, and knows not the utmost that vice promises to her followers, and rejects it, is but a blank virtue, not a pure; her whiteness is but an excremental whiteness...." Milton understood the high and sublime resonance of the antinomies of the human heart requires a free forum that allows the exercise of the unfettered, God-given conscience of humankind....

* * *

Plato, *The Republic*, Parable of the Cave:

In like manner, when anyone by dialectic attempts through discourse of reason apart from all perceptions of sense to find his way to the very essence of each thing.... he arrives at the limit of the intelligible, as the other in our parable came to the goal of the visible....

And may we not also declare that nothing less than the power of dialectic could reveal this, and that only to one experienced in the studies we have described....

Do you agree, then, said I, that we have set dialectic above all other studies to be as it were the coping stone....

And it is also, said I, the chief test of the dialectic nature and its opposite. For he who can view things in their connection is a dialectician; he who cannot, is not....

* * *

When it comes to any type of scholarly or literary work that truly attempts to probe and break new ground, the freedom of conscience of the writer is absolutely essential. Scholarly and literary history is rife with examples of one generation attempting to suppress the new and progressive views and style of the next wave. Convention and revolt is a literary commonplace that attempts to express this phenomenon of human spiritual evolution.... To suppress such antinomies, as say the Soviets routinely tried to do, only leads the most endowed souls to find other ways or outlets for expressing their God-given conscience, their consciousness of what it means to be a human being, and so on, as in samsidat, now the electronic Internet. Only tyrannical, criminal regimes ever feel the need to coerce human conscience—look what happened to Baha'u'llah Himself under the Ottomans.... Predictably, the censors are always the most contemptibly narrow, rigid little characters with no real ability or creativity....

* * *

"It appears that my oeuvre is Christian and even (practically) irreproachable according to the criteria of Catholic theology. I am not so sure, though I like to hear this. Certainly, it stands out against the background of twentieth century poetry, also Polish poetry, which is agnostic or atheist. Yet the religious content of my poems is not the result of design by a believer; it grew out of my doubts, turmoil, and despair, as they searched for a form. If not for a strong heretical seasoning, the religious content would not have been there. Thus, my resistance to being squeezed into the rubric of 'Catholic poet' was well founded."

—Czeslaw Milosz, *Road-side Dog*

* * *

Frodo:

But I have been too deeply hurt, Sam. I tried to save the Shire, and it has been saved, but not for me. It must often be so, Sam, when things are in danger; some one has to give them up, lose them, so that others may keep them. But you are my heir.... —J.R.R. Tolkien

* * *

"The Prolific and the Devourer: the Artist and the Politician. Let them realise that they are enemies, i.e., that each has a vision of the world which must remain incomprehensible to the other. But let them also realise that they are both necessary and complementary, and further, that there are good and bad politicians, good and bad artists, and that the good must learn to recognise and to respect the good."
—W. H. Auden, *The Prolific and the Devourer*

* * *

"To the Devourer it seems as if the producer was in his chains: but it is not so, he only takes portions of existence and fancies in the whole."

"But the Prolific would cease to be Prolific unless the Devourer, as a sea, received the excess of his delights."

"These two classes of men are always upon earth, and they should be enemies: whoever tries to reconcile them seeks to destroy existence." —William Blake, *The Marriage of Heaven and Hell*

* * *

April 27, 1999
Juan,

Not kind nor generous but honest. *Modernity & the Millenium* is a brilliant reading of the historical Baha'u'llah and the forces that helped to shape his revelation. It establishes beyond question what a huge variance exists between the Teachings of Baha'u'llah and the distortions the Baha'i administration continues to fob off today on Baha'is and non-Baha'is.

Actually, I wrote an essay on Hayden a few years ago but have been unable to find a journal willing to publish it since his thinking on spirituality and race are very far indeed from the prevailing postmodern clichés and, for that matter, the one-dimensional thinking of the UHJ....

I too believe it is part of God's wisdom to have mutilated the UHJ, restricting it to only legislative matters, though they continue to transgress on the consciences of avowed believers and others. You say at the end of your article that "There is room for optimism about the future." I must disagree with you. I really can't believe the future holds much promise for the Baha'i Faith or the UHJ. The many abuses during the last decade show how flawed the institution is and how extreme the measures are to which it is willing to go to retain a kind of tyranny over people's minds and souls that Baha'u'llah himself denounced, as you document so well in your book and articles. These tensions and antinomies will prove lasting ones for the Baha'i Faith, as they are for the human soul....

I do concur that public opinion is now the only recourse for counterbalancing the tyranny of the UHJ. If it is going to lie to people in general, as well as to elected government officials, about the nature of the Baha'i Faith and its practices, there should be consequences. If it won't engage and answer direct questions or appeals, it should have to hear the same questions from the sources of intelligent social opinion that it seeks ultimately to deceive and seduce into its ranks. If I have learnt anything during the more than two-year battle for talk.religion.bahai, it is that driving everything into the open for people to judge and decide for themselves is the only way to handle the outright lies and deceptions that are now routine in Baha'i circles.

* * *

"I, too, had to face the savage personal attacks by my former comrades that were designed to warn others to remain within the fold." —David Horowitz, *Radical Son*

* * *

I want that dynamism of the human soul to have the free rein God has given it in order to unleash its antinomies, allowing room enough to exist to bring in the masses.... thereby sweeping the money changers out of the temple....

* * *

Shakespeare's drama is perhaps the fullest expression of what I mean....

Prospero:

Now my charms are all o'erthrown,
And what strength I have's mine own,
Which is most faint....
But release me from my bands,
With the help of your good hands.
Gentle breath of yours my sails
Must fill, or else my project fails,
Which was to please. Now I want
Spirits to enforce, art to enchant;
And my ending is despair
Unless I be relieved by prayer,
Which pierces so, that it assaults
Mercy itself, and frees all faults.
As you from crimes would pardoned be,
Let your indulgence set me free.

To the UHJ

March 31, 1997

The Universal House of Justice of the Bahais of the World

Haifa, Israel

Dear Members of the Universal House of Justice:

After careful reflection and prayer for the past few days, I've decided that open public discussion and knowledge are more important than my own status as a Bahai.

I have been a Bahai for more than twenty years, since 1976. I became a Bahai by reading almost every single Bahai book published at the time. Given my background as a Catholic and poet, I was deeply moved by the beauty and profundity of the Bahai Writings. As a young person, I spent two months travel teaching throughout Michigan with several other youthful, innocent Bahais. Like many, I have sacrificed financially to contribute to the Bahai Faith. I pioneered for a year and a half in Japan, for two years on an American Indian reservation, and have travel taught in China. The spiritual profundity of the Bahai vision, as reflected in the work of the African-American poet Robert Hayden, inspired me to study at the University of Michigan under him and to spend considerable time and labor editing his collected poems and prose for Liveright and the University of Michigan Press. I have published two essays in the Bahai magazine *World Order* and spent more time than I can remember at Bahai summer camps, workshops, and deepenings. Throughout all my varied Bahai experience, I have loved the Figures and Teachings of the Faith even as the conviction has grown that all information and discussion in the Bahai Faith is subtly manipulated, controlled, and distorted for the "good of the Faith." There seems to be a pervasive, rigid control of all thought, ideas, and information that calls into question the motives of the individuals in power in the Bahai Administration.

As a published writer and former college and university instructor of rhetoric and literature for over ten years, I believe the whole process of "review" has become a complete farce and disgrace to the Bahai Faith and is suggestive of the worst censorship under the most repressive regimes, religious or secular, of historical experience. If one truly wishes to understand why many Bahais, both highly educated and others, leave the Bahai Faith or become "inactive" and withdraw into silence and uninvolvement with the religion, one need only to look objectively at what seems to be the oppressive and coercive methods of people in the Bahai Administration itself to find the answer.

My experiencing of these same methods of censorship and distortion on soc.religion.bahai proved to be the last intolerable straw. My attempt to form an unmoderated newsgroup on the Internet that no one could manipulate and censor has a long experience of Bahai tyranny in the background. The resorting to deceit and back-channel communication by the moderators of soc.religion.bahai and others naively believing they're working for the benefit of the Bahai Faith by campaigning for 691 unethical NO votes on talk.religion.bahai further proves the pervasive acceptance of disreputable tactics by Bahais in their attempt to maintain a stranglehold over all thought and discussion.

Recently, more than ever, I've often recalled the words to me in private several times of Robert Hayden, the only Bahai to be appointed Consultant in Poetry to the Library of Congress: "Why I continue to have anything to do with the Bahai Faith, I do not know, I do not know." I myself no longer know. I suppose I hope that the oppressive, coercive methods that have come to be accepted and justified in the Bahai Administration, demonstrated for instance in the crushing of the magazine *Dialogue*, the incidents surrounding the Bahai Encyclopedia, the listserv Talisman I, and the continuingly crude, unreadable propaganda vehicle of *The American Bahai*, might yet be put aside in favor of the beautiful vision of Baha'u'llah and Abdul-Baha for freedom of religious conscience and belief and a humane, tolerant universalism. I fear that all too often the religious totalitarianism of Baha'u'llah's fanatical homeland has seeped into every nook and cranny of His religion, smothering out the free light of the human soul and hamstringing His Administration.

It was with the bitterest of feelings that I observed some time ago the Bahai exhibition, a deceitful propaganda event really, on freedom of religious conscience and belief sponsored by the National Spiritual Assembly in the rotunda of the Capitol in Washington, D.C., so far in reality from the truth was it, so misled, trusting, and uninformed were the Congressmen of my country....

If censorship is allowed in the Bahai Faith, I would like to know what passages of the Bahai Writings support it and what are the "rules," if you will, of Bahai censorship. It seems to me that censorship pervades the Bahai Faith so thoroughly that some Bahais regularly use it as a method of intimidation and silencing of anyone with an unconventional opinion by accusing the individual of being a covenant breaker. This tactic was used against me by at least three Bahais during the discussion period for talk.religion.bahai and tacitly condoned by the moderators and others.

I include, at the end, a threatening, coercive email message I received on March 27, 1997, from Mr. Hoda Mahmoudi, Auxiliary Board Member for Michigan, at a crucial juncture of the discussion and voting for talk.religion.bahai and would like an explanation of his motives.

I, and perhaps the rest of the world, would greatly appreciate evidence that there are not now nine ayatollahs residing in Israel on Mt Carmel.

Respectfully, Frederick Glaysher

95 Theses of the Reform Bahai Faith

To His Great Ends, the Reform Bahai Faith invites all souls to a Convocation of celebration, brotherhood, and Reform, during Ridvan, 2006.

The Reform Bahai Faith, calling to mind the sufferings and imprisonment of the Bab, Baha'u'llah, and Abdul-Baha, under the brutal oppression of tyrannical regimes, bent upon silencing and destroying their testimony of God's New Day, resolves

1. To witness the truth of the deviation of the organized, incorporated Baha'i Faith from the Path, and its imposition of manifest corruptions and innovations, over many lamentable decades, that have wrought ever-increasing alienation, fear, censorship, coercion, misrepresentation, distortion, and damage, all the stratagems of despots and dictators, political and religious, upon individual Bahais, their families, and the community of believers.

2. To seek afresh His Will, as at the dawn of a New Day, whereby the earth is born anew and man stands transparent before God's manifestation of His Will.

3. Baha'u'llah execrated execration, slander, and abuse, shunned shunning, and warned his followers against such unseemly tactics.

4. He prohibited the burning of books and all its evils.

5. The tongue and the pen are the sword of this Day.

6. Liberty was a Teaching of Baha'u'llah, recognized and respected by His Son, Abdul-Baha.

7. Baha'u'llah envisions a spiritual democracy.

8. The Founders of the Bahai Dispensation teach a Universal Religion.

9. The Founders did not teach a system of stifling rules and regulations.

10. Crippling creeds of the soul and conscience are abominations.

11. The Writings of Baha'u'llah teach freedom of conscience and respect for the individual.

12. Assemblies are servants of the Bahai community, not dictatorships that are designed to hector people into submission and servile obedience.

13. At all levels, subtle manipulation of the voting for assemblies has undermined and destroyed the integrity of Baha'i "administration."

14. A free, open, and honest voting system, allowing for the give and take of the qualities of individuals, is essential for service to His Cause.

15. The Founders taught not an organization but a Faith.

16. Persecution, harassment, and enmity are barred from the tabernacle of religious freedom.

17. Baha'u'llah did not "copyright" His Revelation but gave it freely to all the peoples of the earth.

18. The more than 3,000 martyrs did not die for a trademark and copyright.

19. Slander and libel, as well as all their variations, are

anathema in the Writings of Baha'u'llah.

20. Legalism is the dead letter of the atrophied spirit.

21. The Ocean of His Revelation beckons all mankind to dive and swim in it, seeking its pearls of Wisdom.

22. Shoghi Effendi's death ended the era of an authorized interpreter of Baha'u'llah's Revelation.[1]

23. Shoghi Effendi did not appoint anyone, directly or indirectly, to succeed him as Guardian.

24. The Universal House of Justice has only legislative power, not interpretive.

25. Baha'u'llah opened His House of Worship to all mankind at all times and all conditions.

26. Baha'u'llah's Universal Revelation transcends the locks and chains created after the passing of the Master.

27. Reform Bahais make no claim to possess His Truth but seek it everywhere and always.

28. His Revelation is not a means for a disguised sacerdotal order to acquire material and monetary wealth and control.

29. His Revelation is a call to service, sacrifice, and

---

[1] The Reform Bahai Articles depart from this acceptance, in the 95 Theses and On Bahai Liberty, of the authenticity of the will and testament of Abdul-Baha and the legitimacy of a guardian. See the Reform Bahai Articles and Abdul-Baha's *Address upon the Covenant*.

brotherhood.

30. All portions of the Bahai Feast are open for the repast of humanity.

31. God's Gift to all mankind is the Most Great Name.

32. Deceiving the governments of the earth, East and West, and the United Nations, playing them off against one another, misleading their appointed and elected officials and representatives, is a despicable practice.

33. The financial and accounting records for the support of Bahai "administrators" or clergy shall be open and freely available for review by members and the general public.

34. Baha'u'llah did not reveal a declaration of trust and by-laws.

35. The Bahai Spirit loathes creeds and obscurantism.

36. Baha'u'llah's Call is to Unity and Love: "Consort with the followers of all religions."

37. Ecclesiasticism and dogmas are the structure of division, abuse, and exploitation.

38. Baha'u'llah suffered for freedom of conscience.

39. Abdul-Baha taught, "The Bahai Cause is not an organization."

40. Reform Bahais do not seek "the elimination of any non-Bahai views."

41. Abdul-Baha taught it is necessary and acceptable that

citizens participate in the affairs of their nation.

42. Baha'u'llah and Abdul-Baha invoked openness to all of humankind, not Religious Isolation.

43. Social Isolation is the control tactic of tyrants and despots, charlatans and cults, fearfully dominating their flock.

44. Fund raising is not an end in itself but a means of service to the people.

45. The Goal of the Founders was not world domination but attainment to the knowledge of God and service to one's fellow man.

46. God's gift to humankind is a liberal and lofty Cause, conserving the spiritual heritage of humanity.

47. No form of the destruction of the press is taught and tolerated.

48. A membership card does not record the testimony of the heart.

49. No man or organization can fathom the depths God has freely bestowed upon the human heart.

50. At all heights, the bird of humanity soars upon two wings.

51. Baha'u'llah and Abdul-Baha taught independent investigation of the Truth.

52. Abdul-Baha taught "conscientious opinion" and "freedom of conscience, liberty of thought, and right of speech."

53. The literal interpretation of Abdul-Baha's Will and

Testament has profoundly damaged Baha'u'llah's Faith and destroyed countless lives and Bahai communities.

54. Thought-police, under any name, are not included in Baha'u'llah's Vision.

55. Baha'u'llah's Dispensation does not include boards of censorship.

56. Baha'u'llah's model for His New World Order is not the tyrannical religious institutions of the past.

57. Bahai community life is not based on organized totalitarianism.

58. Charitable works have more value in the sight of God than marbled ostentation.

59. Fear is the refuge of tyrants and their primary crutch.

60. The Reform Bahai Faith places its trust in God.

61. Spying, informing, and keeping files and records on people for matters of conscience and opinion, expressed on or off the Internet, in email or any other form, are all denounced and banned.

62. Reform Bahais embrace loving association with all the peoples of the earth and do not require identity checks, letters, and cards of verification.

63. The nine doors of fraternity are open to all human beings.

64. The nine doors are open at all times.

65. Segregation and indoctrination, individually or

collectively, are contrary to the Writings of Baha'u'llah.

66. Excommunication is excommunicated.

67. The practices of the Middle Ages are history and are an instructive lesson before which Reform Bahais beg God for guidance and protection.

68. The Soul's Covenant is with God and Baha'u'llah.

69. Abdul-Baha taught, "The conscience of man is sacred and to be respected."

70. Everywhere in His Writings, Baha'u'llah loathes injustice, tyranny, and oppression.

71. Guilt by association and collective punishment have no place in Baha'u'llah's Dispensation.

72. A self-serving clergy, hiding behind the secular nuances of the word "administration," remains a pack of wolves whatever the clothing and outward seeming.

73. Non-Bahais and Bahais have the human right to know the fullness of the historical record, without concealment and revision.

74. Abdul-Baha taught human rights are Bahai rights.

75. The distortion and corruption of historical fact is detrimental to the development of humanity and of Baha'u'llah's Faith.

76. "The Bahai Technique" is not Baha'u'llah's.

77. Individual conscience is not a "dangerous delusion out of

Christianity" but a glorious gift of God.

78. Baha'u'llah taught moderation in all things.

79. Abdul-Baha taught humility before one's convictions.

80. Intellectual vigor, especially of the young, should never be crushed, but nurtured.

81. The descendants of the Bab and Baha'u'llah have no special or hereditary prerogatives and rights.

82. Abdul-Baha set the requirements for Bahai membership: "To be a Bahai simply means to love all the world; to love humanity and try to serve it; to work for universal peace and universal brotherhood."

83. Bahais may associate with people of all religious persuasions.

84. Receipt of mail or communication is not mandatory.

85. Harassment for declining the receipt of mail is prohibited and in all cases rejected.

86. Membership statistics are free and open to all interested parties.

87. Shoghi Effendi's writings indisputably contain errors.

88. Bahai experience and history demonstrate that the organized Baha'i Faith has strayed from Baha'u'llah's Teachings and blindly and fanatically opposes all discussion and Reformation.

89. Bahais of good conscience have no alternative but to

recognize reality and restore and Reform, at all levels, His Teachings.

90. The Reform Bahai Faith looks not to other Bahai denominations for its understanding of Baha'u'llah's Teachings.

91. The Reform Bahai Faith looks to the fullness of Baha'u'llah's Revelation for guidance.

92. The Reform Bahai Faith does not distort nor select single or unusual passages of the Writings to manipulate or over-emphasize for organizational purposes of thought-control and indoctrination.

93. The Reform Bahai Faith trusts and allows the individual believer to pray and meditate on the inner meaning and purpose of His Revelation, sharing the fruits of reflection with all who are willing to hear, receive, and discuss, without disgraceful groveling or humiliating qualifications.

94. The Reform Bahai Faith recognizes and formalizes the inescapable conflicts of the human spirit that have existed in Baha'u'llah's Faith since the passing of the Master, exacerbated by an oppressive and inflexible interpretation of Baha'u'llah's Teachings.

95. The Reform Bahai Faith rejoices at the Glory of His Revelation and seeks to share His Teachings, with unabashed and renewed enthusiasm, for the Redemption and Renewal of the human race.

Baha'u'llah called all humanity to feast at His bounteous Table.

Reform Bahais rejoice that God has revealed, through time

and history, the inevitable path, through trial and turmoil, toward fulfillment of His Vision.

The Reform Bahai Faith invites all non-Bahais, Bahais, ex-Bahais, all humanity, the tens of thousands of people harassed and driven out by fanatical extremists, maligned and slandered, to join together in His Worship and in service to humanity, to restore a sane and moderate form of community life and association based on love, trust, and brotherhood, across all barriers of race and division, social and economic, nationalistic and provincial.

The Reform Bahai Faith bows humbly before His Threshold, supplicating for His Favor and Guidance, supplicating the Hosts of the Kingdom of Abha, recognizing the difficulties and obstacles, apparent and hidden, that confront and will confront the realization of His Vision.

To His Great Ends, the Reform Bahai Faith invites all souls to a Convocation of celebration, brotherhood, and Reform, during Ridvan, 2006.

August 19, 2004

On Bahai Liberty

The Prisoner of Akka, Baha'u'llah, lived much of His life deprived of liberty, harassed and suppressed by the tyranny of one despot or another, yet He envisions a world of global freedom and universal brotherhood. From His experience of the liberty of His own Mind, from His mystical experience of the oneness of God, He teaches the oneness of all religions and the oneness of humankind. His immortal and challenging proclamation is "The earth is but one country and mankind its citizens." His love of liberty resonates with the noblest reflections on liberty that run throughout human history, East or West. Like Edmund Burke, Lord Acton, and the signers of the Declaration of Independence, Baha'u'llah upheld a responsible liberty seasoned with a sense of duty to God and society, while preserving and protecting the sanctity of the individual from tyranny and debasement.

What the Baha'i Faith has become today contrasts sharply with His enlightened Writings: a prison house of oppression, coercion, deception, manipulation, employing all manner of "slanderous vilification" against its own members for the slightest ideological divergence from its interpretation of His Teachings, calculated to deprive the individual of religious liberty and freedom of conscience, demanding nothing less than complete, absolute, and servile obedience. From a secular perspective, the Baha'i Faith has become the antitheses of the liberty discussed by John Stuart Mill in his classic work and the antitheses of the virtues extolled by Baha'u'llah and his son in the societies of England and the United States of America.

To those who are unfamiliar with the complicated history of the Baha'i Faith during the last one hundred years, these claims may well seem extreme and unwarranted, if one only knows the version propagated by self-serving Baha'i sources. To those who have suffered at the hands of Baha'i administrative inquisitors and oppressors, these claims will ring all too true, evoking bitter and painful memories. For the past ten to thirty years, the Baha'i Faith has imposed one inquisition after another upon its members. It has been widely assumed by many Baha'is that these incidents marked a temporary aberration from Baha'i administrative conduct, which would soon be corrected once the Universal House of Justice became sufficiently apprised of the issues involved, and that it would reprimand the particular counselor or auxiliary board member involved. Time has gone by, and incident after incident has accumulated, bringing home to many that far from a temporary aberration, a prison house of tyranny has indeed supplanted the liberty of the individual mind and soul that Baha'u'llah and Abdul-Baha had guaranteed their followers.

It is the sheer number of these incidents that convey, more than any one of them, the truest picture of what has become of Baha'u'llah's Faith. In the mid 1970s, a group of young students and scholars in Los Angeles loosely formed a study class for the sharing and encouragement of their research of Baha'i history and theology. They were harangued, harassed, and attacked, some leaving the Baha'i Faith in confusion and disbelief. Later in that decade, Baha'i scholars at the University of Michigan and elsewhere who were commissioned, by the National Spiritual Assembly of the United States of America, to write a Baha'i encyclopedia, met with a similar experience, many ending up having to resign from working on it, believing they could not do so in good conscience, given the interference of Baha'i authorities regarding historical fact and detail; some were driven out into the self-censorship of silence. The 1980s witnessed an increasing number of incidents. In 1987 "A Modest Proposal," intended for, but never published, in *Dialogue Magazine*, attempted to suggest improvements in procedure and operation of the national community, only to be publicly denounced at the national convention the following year, while its writers were handled in a most reprehensible fashion, some threatened with excommunication. Another group of scholars and writers in 1998 contributed to a paper known as "The Service of Women" which again met with a vehement crackdown all out of proportion to the issues and intentions of its authors. No brief highlighting of the shockingly dictatorial abuse of power by the Baha'i administration would be complete without mention of an open letter in 1996 by Steven Scholl, one of the *Dialogue* editors, which attempted to bring attention to the frequency and severity of these incidents and urged moderation and a more open and tolerant community. Many of the young editors and writers of *Dialogue Magazine*, as well as others, have been harassed and hounded into silence or driven out the door.

With the wide availability and development of the Internet during the 1990s, Baha'is all around the world, enjoying the liberty given them by God Himself and lauded by both Baha'u'llah and Abdul-Baha, entered into free and open discussion in a number of online venues. One of the first was Talisman, an email list sponsored through one scholar's affiliation with Indiana University. Baha'i interrogators of conscience were quick to quibble and denounce members for their views and opinions expressed in emails to group members, ultimately denouncing, as had happened in previous incidents, individuals as "covenant breakers" or possibly holding opinions which were tending toward covenant breaking. Through such methods, the abuse of individuals was carried out "in the best interest of the Faith," driving more young, intelligent, inquisitive, vigorous minds and souls away in shock and horror over what the Baha'i Faith had become, not was.

Another major incident, publicly documented in the newsgroup databases of Google and other search engines, was the proposal of an open and unmoderated newsgroup, talk.religion.bahai. Given the pervasive censorship and manipulation of thought and discussion on the previously existing newsgroup, soc.religion.bahai, praised in *The American Baha'i*, many Baha'is and non-Baha'i observers believed such a newsgroup was essential for unfettered discussion about Baha'i matters of concern. The overwhelming opposition of Baha'is to its formation shocked many inside and outside of the Baha'i

Faith, as many fundamentalists called upon Baha'is "in good standing" and "firm in the covenant" to vote NO against it, garnering more than 600 votes through such rabble-rousing techniques on private Baha'i-only email lists. It took two years and three rounds of voting to create what is still, as of 2004, the only forum on the Internet that cannot technically prevent the expression of any opinion or point of view.

No survey of incidents should fail to mention the lawsuit of Deborah Buchhorn against the National Spiritual Assembly of the Baha'is of the United States and the Assembly of Albuquerque, New Mexico for fraud and libel in 2001. The court's dismissal of the lawsuit proved only that the government of the United States was wisely not about to adjudicate on issues of religion and conscience and in no way exonerated the Baha'i administration of the charges.

Throughout all these incidents and others, most Baha'is thought only in terms of an aberration, surely something had gone wrong, a miscarriage of Baha'i justice that the ultimate defender of justice, the Universal House of Justice, would rectify, restoring order and sanity to Baha'u'llah's Cause. Yet the tactics used were virtually identical in each case, and have become widely known, through talk.religion.bahai, as "The Baha'i Technique," essentially, "slanderous vilification," imputations of covenant breaking or incipient covenant breaking, frightening people involved into silence, fear, and self-censorship. To assist in this program of ideological terrorization of the Baha'i community, the uhj has on a number of occasions apparently, or purportedly, autocratically thrown people out of the Baha'i Faith, despite such a practice not existing anywhere in the Baha'i Writings, despite Shoghi Effendi explicitly stating that only the Guardian could pronounce someone a covenant breaker. This indefensible, desperate tactic, non-doctrinal, has been wielded a number of times since 1997. All these incidents and more are documented on the Internet and elsewhere for those unfamiliar with them or for those who wish to independently investigate them further: http://www.fglaysher.com/bahaicensorship/

How often in religious history have the teachings and vision of the Founder become debased by the organization that rears itself upon His Sacrifice. No impartial, fair-minded observer who conscientiously explores, to whatever degree, these incidents, thus far recounted, can fail to perceive that the Baha'i Faith and what it calls its "administrative order" has become, in the most apropos words of Martin Luther, a "terrible tyranny." Its wolves in sheep's clothing have turned far aside from the Middle Path, envisioned by Baha'u'llah and Abdul-Baha, universally condoned by the reason of all persuasions. On all sides Baha'i administrators see only heretics and apostates, point the finger, denounce people as breakers of Baha'u'llah's covenant, or Abdul-Baha's Will and Testament, or Shoghi Effendi's non-existent will, which, in disobedience to Abdul-Baha, he never wrote.

In 2004, H-Net, a scholarly website supported by Michigan State University and Humanities & Social Sciences Online, reprinted in digital format the works of Mirza Ahmad Sohrab, who for over eight years served Abdul-Baha as a secretary and translator in the Middle East and on his American and European journeys. In Sohrab's several books, especially in *Broken Silence: The Story of Today's Struggle for Religious Freedom* (1942) and *The Will and Testament of Abdul-Baha: An Analysis* (1944), Sohrab presents his opinion that the Baha'i Faith was already well on the road to becoming an oppressive organization in the 1920s and '30s, exploitative of the individual, and departing further, with every year, from the moderation and predominately democratic liberalism of Baha'u'llah and Abdul-Baha. Sohrab located the source of the emerging problems of conscience and religious freedom in the desire of some early American Baha'is for absolute control, modeled on the Roman Catholic Church and other forms of autocratic religious organization, leading to and encouraging Shoghi

Effendi's increasingly fanatical interpretation of Abdul-Baha's Will and Testament:

> To interpret this section of the Will in such a literal sense, is, to say the least, utterly short-sighted and a complete subversion of all the glorious teachings of the Bahai Cause (53).

The young and impressionable Shoghi Effendi, a little dreamy and not entirely ready for it all, unsure of himself and what direction to chart after Abdul-Baha's passing, increasingly came under the influence of people in both the East and West who wanted a rigidly controlled bureaucratic system, until his own hand became the dominating force shaping the now trademarked, incorporated, and copyrighted organization. H-Net's digital reprinting brought home for insightful observers of the victimization of fellow Baha'is, during the purges and pogroms of the 1970s and after, the inescapable realization that, far from an aberration, the same pervasive fanaticism and censorship had indeed been experienced by Sohrab and earlier Baha'is in virtually the same form and manner. No amount of distorting and slandering the intentions and beliefs of Sohrab and Mrs. Chanler could deny the validity and eloquent truth of their own testimony, repeated and confirmed by the experience of subsequent generations of Baha'is.

Dying without leaving a will in 1957, Shoghi Effendi left the Baha'i Faith with no infallible successor, no appointed Guardian, and no infallible interpreter of Baha'u'llah's Writings. Shoghi Effendi's own words state emphatically that without a Guardian the Baha'i Faith would be mutilated and completely deprived of the "unerring guidance of God." Subsequent to his death, Baha'i experience only corroborates his judgment. No matter to what extent the Hands of the Cause assumed, or presumed, an authority that neither Abdul-Baha's Will and Testament nor any of the writings of Shoghi Effendi bestowed, their innovations and attempts to lay a credible foundation for the uhj failed, and time has proven it, made it open and blatant as the noonday sun.

The end of the Guardianship and the innovations and attempts to fill in the gaps and unfulfilled portions of Abdul-Baha's Will and Testament have continued unabated since the earliest schism between the Hands of the Cause, their unilateral and unauthorized attempt to fill the interpretive void left by Shoghi Effendi's failure to foresee his untimely end and the commotions it would unleash upon Baha'u'llah's Faith. Neither the custodians nor the Orthodox Baha'is had, or have, a credible claim to assumption of the mantle of authority. Nothing in Abdul-Baha's Will and Testament nor Shoghi Effendi's writings anticipated or justified what they did after the Guardian's death. Similarly, the International Baha'i Council that the Hands put aside was not in the Will and Testament nor an instrument of the Master for the appointment of a new Guardian. That the Hands were nominated and appointed by Shoghi Effendi gave them no legitimate authority to assume, or usurp, the "rights and powers in succession to the Guardian," which they claimed, nor to change the method of creating a universal house of justice from what was stipulated by the Master in His Will and was already anticipated by the Guardian through the unfolding of the International Baha'i Council. Any pretense to "infallibility" ended with Shoghi Effendi, and subsequent Baha'i experience has proven it in the ruined and destroyed lives of many thousands of individuals, married couples, families, and Baha'i communities.

The eventual creation by the uhj of the continental board of counselors, a type of Baha'i college of cardinals, and the auxiliary boards, notorious for operating like the Jesuits at their worst, has only exacerbated the situation and deepened the rift between Baha'is in all walks of life and the barely concealed clergy that now exists and demands at every turn "obedience" to the covenant, as the "infallible" universal house of justice interprets it, ignoring that Abdul-Baha and Shoghi Effendi both explicitly stated that only the Guardian has interpretive guidance and that the uhj has only legislative authority.

For decades the fanatical interpretation of Abdul-Baha's Will and Testament has demonstrated that not the slightest reform, or suggestion of reform, will be tolerated, let alone considered or acted upon. The uhj and its clergy have demonstrated beyond a doubt that they do not possess infallible powers or interpretive authority worthy of respect, let alone obedience.

Reform Bahais have watched or participated in all this. Many have been victims of intolerance and witch hunts; of coercion of conscience and denunciation, ostracism and shunning, and all the other tactics and techniques of "The Baha'i Technique," suffered under the ferocious attacks of their fellow Baha'is who never hesitate to violate the Words of Abdul-Baha: "According to the direct and sacred command of God we are forbidden to utter slander."

Far from censuring such slander, a corrupted organization has encouraged among its cadre an ever more vicious campaign of slander, by what Mirza Ahmad Sohrab rightly recognized and scathingly called in the 1940s, "fawning, cringing, sniveling, mealy-mouthed sycophants, flatterers and flunkies."

Lessoned by time and history, by experience that cannot be taken but as a revelation of the Will of God, an unveiling of what lies behind the marble facade, acknowledging that the loss of the dream of unity and infallibility happened long ago, Reform Bahais seek to recover, restore, and return to Baha'u'llah's central and pristine Teachings—the oneness of God, the oneness of religion, the oneness of humankind—to His vision of responsible individual liberty in service to humanity, to the Example of the Master's Love, Wisdom, Kindness, Compassion, and Self-Sacrifice.

Reform Bahais choose to leave those who choose hatred, denunciation, shunning, endless and unproductive argument and recrimination over Abdul-Baha's Will and Testament, seeking justification for fanaticism, over the Will of Shoghi Effendi, which he never wrote or implied, or over the successors he never intended or appointed, or over the oppressive organization Baha'u'llah Himself never envisioned nor proclaimed.

Reform Bahais invite all Bahais, all humanity, to a Convocation of celebration, peace, love, and brotherhood, to seek humbly His Will, during Ridvan 2006.

October 4, 2004

Reform Bahai Articles

To be a Bahai simply means to love all the world; to love humanity and try to serve it; to work for universal peace and universal brotherhood.
—Abdul-Baha

For over three years now since 2004, the Reform Bahai Faith has once again existed, born anew from tyranny and oppression, from essentially the same spiritual upheavals as that of Ruth White, Mirza Ahmad Sohrab, Julie Chanler, and the thousands of Bahais who left in protest under the imposition of an oppressive organization based on the fraudulent will and testament of Abdul-Baha throughout the 1920s, '30s, and '40s. God has, throughout the decades, preserved the historical record of events for perceptive minds and souls.

Despite all fanatical, fundamentalist attempts to suppress all memory of Abdul-Baha's vision and interpretation of Baha'u'llah's Faith, to root it out, to coerce and slander, malign and expell, shun and besmirch the testimony of the Writings and the early believers, the Bahai Movement has continued to endure, quietly persist, giving testimony to the vision of God's oneness, the oneness of humanity and religion, and the human potential for peace and brotherly love.

The books and publications of White, Sohrab, and Chanler have kept this vision alive, while the Baha'i upheavals and conflicts of the last three decades have led many thousands of Baha'is to experience for themselves the depth and degree to which the Faith of Baha'u'llah has been traduced and desecrated by people who seek to use and exploit it for their own worldly benefit, power, glory, and material gain.

The Divine Being has created a world of impermanence, evanescence, where nothing lasts forever, and all humanity is subjected to the vicissitudes of life, the fragility of health and constitution, the limits of human existence that He alone knows and sets. With an increasing sense of mortality, I feel it is incumbent upon me to set down, in writing, my own testimony of what I believe to be the truth about the Bahai Faith, having now been a member for over thirty years and having watched or participated in many struggles and debates and studied or watched those of many other souls in their search for truth and understanding.

Thinking of Martin Luther and John Wesley, I feel it especially as a duty and obligation to leave a record of my views for the Reform Bahai Convocation, which, God willing, one day, shall convene to restore and revive the moderate, spiritual religion of Baha'u'llah and Abdul-Baha and clearly set a new course away from the fanatical and fundamentalist Shiite sect of the Haifans, based on their fraudulent will and testament, propagating a manipulative creed intended only to coerce the individual believer and subject him or her to the tyranny of an illegitimate and mutilated organization.

Article I

"The Revelation which, from time immemorial, hath been acclaimed as the Purpose and Promise of all the Prophets of God, and the most cherished Desire of His Messengers, hath now, by virtue of the pervasive Will of the Almighty and at His irresistible bidding, been revealed unto men. The advent of such a Revelation hath been heralded in all the sacred Scriptures."

—Baha'u'llah

Article II

Baha'u'llah's appointed heir and interpreter is Abdul-Baha.

Article III

As scientifically judged by Dr. C. Ainsworth Mitchell, the purported will and testament of Abdul-Baha is a fraudulent document: "That is to say, the writing does not agree with the hypothesis that it was all written by one person." "A minute comparison of the authenticated writing with the writing on every page of the alleged will . . . has failed to detect in any part of the will the characteristics of the writing of Abdul-Baha, as shown in the authenticated specimens." Dr. C. Ainsworth Mitchell, *Report on the Writing Shown on the Photographs of the Alleged Will of Abdul-Baha*, Library of Congress, 1930.

Article IV

The Baha'i organizations, based upon the fraudulent document, including the writings of Shoghi Effendi, are inescapably defective and deficient: "There is apparent contradiction between this section of the Will and his lifelong teachings." "Abdul Baha had never in speech or writing given the slightest indication that there would be a successor to himself. On the contrary, a number of addresses delivered by him on various occasions had made the opposite impression." Mirza Ahmad Sohrab, *The Will and Testament of Abdul Baha: An Analysis*. New York: Universal Publishing, 1944 (61).

Article V

The results of the spurious document has reverberated down the generations and decades, as Ruth White rightly perceived: **"Whether the alleged will of Abdul Baha is authentic or spurious, the results of the administration of Shoghi Effendi and the National Spiritual Assembly of Baha'is stand as an historical indictment against them.** [Boldface in original] They no more represent the Bahai Religion than the bigots of the dark ages of Christianity." Ruth White. *Abdul Baha's Questioned Will and Testament*. Beverly Hills: White, 1946 (100).

Article VI

"The Bahai Movement is not an organization. You cannot organize the Bahai Movement." —Abdul-Baha. The mystery of that paradox calls all Bahais to seek its meaning and return to the universal, liberal Teachings of Baha'u'llah and Abdul-Baha and their Writings.

Article VII

Far from creating a theocratic tyranny, the Founders of the Bahai Faith taught a moderate, universal, global religion, grounded in a spiritual democracy, teaching the separation of church and state, with science in its own respected domain, each a profound differentiation of social duty and responsibility, as in Abdul-Baha's "Sermon on the Art of Governance":

"The religious law is like the spirit of life,
 the government is the locus of the force of deliverance.
The religious law is the shining sun,
 and government is the clouds of April.
These two bright stars are like twin lights in the heavens of the contingent world,
 they have cast their rays upon the people of the world.
One has illuminated the world of the soul,
 the other has caused the earth to flower.
One sowed pearls in the oceans of conscience,
 while the other has made the surface of the earth a garden of paradise." (Tr. Sen McGlinn)

Article VIII

With every passing year, the Writings of Baha'u'llah are being restored to humanity, from those who debased and lowered them to the level of a trademark and copyright.

Article IX

Reform Bahais choose to leave those who choose hatred, shunning, and interminable recrimination over the fraudulent will and testament and over stultifying legalisms, and look to the Spirit of brotherhood and love, knowledge and understanding, prayer and meditation, worship and community, service to one's country and the world of humanity.

With the assurance of Abdul-Baha that humanity has entered the stage of maturity, wherein the individual can independently search for truth, Reform Bahais testify, in this universal, global age, that He reserves for Himself the "hearts of men," rendering to Caesar what is Caesar's, as Baha'u'llah taught in the *Epistle to the Son of the Wolf*, accepting and embracing His multifaceted vision, the mystery that surpasses understanding.

Reform Bahais invite all Bahais, all humanity, to a Convocation of celebration, peace, love, and brotherhood, to seek humbly together His Will and service, for the good of all people and nations of this spinning globe.

October 4, 2007

Analysis of Abdul-Baha's 1912 Authentic Covenant

Abdul-Baha's 1912 Authentic Covenant
www.reformbahai.org/Covenant.html

Abdul-Baha's Interpretation of Baha'u'llah's Teachings is a broad, open, loving Covenant of God with humanity, and it is articulated in simple language, in his 1912 *Address Upon the Covenant.*[1] It is universal, moderate, predicated on pluralistic spiritual democracy, based on a separation of church and state, not tyranny, and emphasizes the universality, the non-creedal and non-exclusivism of religious truth.

Abdul-Baha delivered his *Address Upon the Covenant*, on June 19, 1912. It was clearly perceived to be important enough at the time to be almost immediately, and repeatedly, published, unlike the majority of Abdul-Baha's addresses that year, yet it was quietly suppressed, just after Abdul-Baha's passing in 1921, when the editing of the 1922 text of *The Promulation of Universal Peace* took place and in subsequent editions. Evidently, it contradicted too much the new theocratic interpretation. In it Abdul-Baha briefly highlights the various covenants of God with humanity, with each Manifestation alluding to His successor. Abdul-Baha makes no mention of a guardian or His "appointing" anyone, least of all Shoghi Effendi.

It was "approved" and published as a pamphlet on November 12, 1912 for the celebration of the Birth of Baha'u'llah, and thereafter at least three times in the *Star of the West*, one of

---

[1] The text and a facsimile of the *Address Upon the Covenant* may be found in the APPENDIX and online at reformbahai.org.

which was a special issue devoted to this Covenant, Abdul-Baha's authentic Covenant. From the pen of Abdul-Baha, no other document ever existed, among Bahais, that was given such prominence prior to his death in 1921.

Paradoxically, contrasted with his other statements that the Bahai Movement could not be "organized," Abdul-Baha clearly indicates some type of organization leading to a Universal House of Justice, but nowhere did he ever suggest Bahai assemblies should become the oppressive and tyrannical "administration" known today for destroying marriages and families through excommunication and shunning and intruding into virtually every aspect of the life and conscience of the individual.

It was such statements and publications as this address that led Mirza Ahmad Sohrab to remark on

> the fact that Abdul Baha had never in speech or writing given the slightest indication that there would be a successor to himself. On the contrary, a number of addresses delivered by him on various occasions had made the opposite impression. Consequently , it took several years before a section of the Bahais could adjust themselves to the new situation *(The Will and Testament of Abdul Baha, An Analysis*, 1944, 61).

Ruth White was one of the early believers who was not about to forget such statements by Abdul-Baha and courageously fought to preserve the actual, authentic Covenant, as taught by Abdul-Baha, versus the fraudulent will and testament passed off on the community by the family of Shoghi Effendi. Neither could some thousands of other early believers "adjust," and many left or were driven out during the next few decades *(Abdul Baha's Questioned Will and Testament*, 1946 11).

Abdul-Baha's conception of the Covenant is not at all like the fanatical, oppressive one imposed by Shoghi Effendi and propped up by "administrators" who believed they knew better than Abdul-Baha, such as Horace Holley and Charles Mason Remey, both of whom were quick not only to "adjust," but zealously supported and promoted the "appointee" of the spurious will and testament, who delegated authority in return back to them. Abdul-Baha clearly never conceived of any successor other than eventually an elected, democratic Universal House of Justice, one definitely without an hereditary guardian analogous to a Shiite imam or a Sunni caliph. Abdul-Baha knew all too well what social oppression and upheavals those systems of organization had led to, which is one reason he always emphasized spiritual democracy, not tyranny.

One of the typical tactics used to suppress and discredit such public, printed statements by Abdul-Baha was and is to claim that the original Persian transcript has not survived, it's only a "pilgrim's note," hearsay, and so on. Similarly, tactics of slander and shunning, Iranian Shiite "takfir," were unleashed relentlessly against Ruth White, Mirza Ahmad Sohrab, Julie Chanler, and anyone able to think and reflect independently for themselves about Abdul-Baha's authentic Covenant, which, again, contains not the slightest suggestion of a so-called guardian:

> After Abdul-Baha—whenever the Universal House of Justice is organized it will ward off differences.

Had the purported will and testament been written, as alleged, by Abdul-Baha in three sections between 1901 and 1908, when Shoghi Effendi was a young child, yet to prove himself worthy, despite subsequent attempts to cast him as a prodigy, Abdul-Baha would have known the contents of his own will and testament in 1912, as he delivered this address. However, the three different hands that Dr. C. Answorth Mitchell of the British Museum attested actually wrote the fraudulent document, not a one of which was Abdul-Baha's, had not and never did name Shoghi Effendi. One should also recall Abdul-Baha's remarks on His own brother's unworthiness to lead the Baha'i community. It is not credible that Abdul-Baha would have taken such a chance on an approximately four-year-old boy, even a family member.

Whether from a rational or spiritual view, given the overwhelming weight of evidence against the authenticity of the purported will and testament, the burden of proof resides with those Bahai denominations that claim its legitimacy, as Ruth White and other Bahais have stated for decades since at least 1929. It is evident in Ruth White's documents deposited with the Library of Congress that Shoghi Effendi and/or others persuaded or bribed, with "baksheesh," the Palestine officials to put the matter aside, common practice especially in the Middle East of the time. Revealing his calculating guilt, Shoghi Effendi instructed the nsa to do nothing to antagonize Ruth White and to avoid the issue, as she relates in her books and documents in the papers she deposited with the Library of Congress. Ruth White perceptively made a crucial observation a long time ago: The chief beneficiary of a fraudulent, unprobated, and unverified will and testament, Shoghi Effendi, TRANSLATES it, if not after writing it or participating in its creation, and then claims it's "authentic," accusing, discrediting, and castigating anyone who asks for proof of its authenticity as someone "seeking power."

It's important to realize that unlike the customary legal procedure for authenticating a will, observed in most countries of the world, the one in question was never proven to be a legitimate instrument. It was merely asserted as such. Shoghi Effendi and others claimed they saw it, read it, and swore it was Abdul-Baha's handwriting. These people were largely Persian Baha'is who all stood to benefit from the fraudulent document. Often the excuse is made that to authentic it now would imply the charges against it are true, so therefore the Haifan Baha'i administration will not allow examination of it except by "true believers," which only serves to perpetuate the deception and crime.

Though perhaps as many as a few thousand Bahais left the faith over the claims of Shoghi Effendi, the majority of the early Bahai community accepted the will and testament on blind belief, as have subsequent generations, who have also been, to no small degree, brainwashed into unquestioning acceptance of its validity. The Bahai "Donation of Constantine" continues to harm the unsuspecting, those who have ceased to search for truth.

If the Haifan Baha'is were ever to allow examination of what they allege to be Abdul-Baha's will and testament, which is highly unlikely, it would certainly be under a controlled and manipulated setting, with individuals or bodies of "experts" selected, in one way or another, to produce the desired verdict. More likely would be a theft, a fire, an explosion, or some other local or national event or upheaval, which would provide the opportunity to sweep the incriminating document, "so tragically," from the annals of history, depriving the believers of Abdul-Baha's "authentic" original, leaving conveniently the body of loyal followers with only Shoghi Effendi's deceptive translation.

On all counts, the will and testament is a fraudulent document, and Shoghi Effendi knew it would never stand up to further scrutiny, as it didn't with Dr. C. Ainsworth Mitchell, an unimpeachable authority still highly regarded in professional forensic circles.

Considering what actual use and purpose Shoghi Effendi's will and testament has been put over the decades, it no longer truly matters whether it was written by Abdul-Baha or not, so thoroughly discredited has it become as a conception and interpretation of Baha'u'llah's Teachings, transmogrifying them into an appallingly tyrannical system of oppression and coercion.

Reading backwards from a fraudulent document is one of the tactics regularly used by its beneficiaries, namely, Shoghi Effendi, his family, and now the denominations that depend on it. It is difficult for Baha'is committed to, and raised in, the theocratic vision to recognize the truth—but it's right there in black and white in Abdul-Baha's 1912 *Address Upon the Covenant* and won't go away, decade after decade.

Unfortunately, the family of Shoghi Effendi, when they forged the will and testament of Abdul-Baha, followed their cultural biases from Iran, instead of the Teachings of Baha'u'llah and the Interpretation of Abdul-Baha. Essentially, they reverted to the Shiite imamate, creating the mirror image of Iranian obedience to the authority of the imam, the imam of the age, which they called a "guardian," believing, in effect, that he's infallible and must be obeyed in all things. Attempts to create a Bahai imamate are contrary to Abdul-Baha's teaching of a properly elected Universal House of Justice, an institution of Bahai spiritual authority, not worldly.

This Address by Abdul-Baha is the evidence that Reform Bahais today can not forget, now come again to light, preserving Abdul-Baha's vision of a universal, moderate, spiritual democracy, and the separation of church and state.

It is only by reading all of, or extensive extracts from, the *Star of the West*, the early newsletter journal of the Bahai Movement, published from 1910 in Chicago, but effectively the news vehicle for Bahais throughout the West, the United States, Canada, and the British Isles, most of the Bahai world of the time, that one can discern that Abdul-Baha's actual conception and Interpretation of Baha'u'llah's Teachings is significantly differently from the distortions of Shoghi Effendi. Though often repudiated and discredited by Haifan Bahais, for obvious reasons if one reflects, the *Star of the West* provides the pristine, universal vision of Abdul-Baha and Baha'u'llah. Abdul-Baha closely followed, shaped, and guided the editing and publishing of the ideas and views expressed in the *Star of the West*, and, it preserves not only what the Bahai Movement was in his Interpretation, but also what he believed it should become.

Abdul-Baha's *Address Upon the Covenant* was first published in *Star of the West*, November 23, 1912, 9-10; again, a mere year later in *Star of the West*, November 23, 1913, p. 234-9;

and just before his death, emphasizing the importance of the 1912 Covenant exactly when Bahais needed to recall Abdul-Baha's guidance the most, in *Star of the West* November 23, 1921. The reader may corroborate independently this publishing history of the *Address Upon the Covenant* since the entire 1912 to 1913 and 1920 to 1921 volumes of *Star of the West* can be download directly from Google Books.

As far back as 1929 early Bahais were publicly emphasizing the importance of the *Address Upon the Covenant*. See Ruth White, Appendix to *Abdul-Baha and the Promised Age*, 1929, and her comments on this passage, bottom of the first page. Also see, *Star of the West*, Vol. VII, No. 15. p. 139: "When the Universal House of Justice is organized...." There might be further valuable documentation in Mahmoud's *Diary* and Afroukhteh's *Memoires*.

For a sample of the universality that Abdul-Baha's Covenant inspired, see Janabe Fazel Mazandarani, *Star of the West*, May 17, 1921, "The Temple of Universal Religion—The Fundamental Oneness of All Existing Faiths." (See other talks on universal religion by Janabe Fazel) For a sample of the method used to subvert the universality of Abdul-Baha's Covenant, see Charles Mason Remey, *Star of the West*, Aug 20, 1921, "Bahai Organization."

Comparing these two articles, it is easy to understand that, along with the 1912 Covenant, the universality of Abdul-Baha's Teaching was already being put aside, before Abdul-Baha had even died, by Charles Mason Remey, Horace Holley, and others intent on creating an organization that concentrated power and control in their and Shoghi Effendi's hands. Directly repudiating Abdul-Baha's repeated statement that the Bahai Movement could not be organized, rejecting his Covenant, expunging the universality he publicly taught his entire life and throughout the West, witnessed by all the early Bahais, attested to by Ruth White and Ahmad Sohrab in their books, both of whom knew him personally, especially Sohrab, Charles Mason Remey assured Bahais in 1921 that they were "a little confused" and that he and others, implicitly Horace Holley and Shoghi Effendi, as would soon become apparent, knew better what Abdul-Baha intended. That their claims were based on a fraudulent will and testament, written by three different hands, not a one of which was Abdul-Baha's, nor bearing his signature, as he repeatedly emphasized was essential to safeguard his Interpretation of Baha'u'llah's Teaching, meant nothing to those who soon succeeded in undermining the universal faith of God, subjecting it to decades of corruption and ineffectuality, disrupting or destroying the lives of countless Bahais over the years, depriving humankind of Baha'u'llah's saving vision of spiritual oneness and universal peace.

Before the decade was out, the subverters of Abdul-Baha's Interpretation of Baha'u'llah's Faith would be fighting amongst themselves, deceiving the authorities at the time in Palestine and the U. S. Copyright Office in 1928, slandering and eventually suing Bahais of other denominations who dared to realize and speak out against the crimes committed against the Bahai Cause (details under Early Reform Bahais on the Reform Bahai website). For the lawsuits of the 1960s and the one beginning in 2006 in the US District Court of Northern Illinois, consult the Internet by Googling "Orthodox Baha'is lawsuit rift."

Compare the repeatedly published and emphasized 1912 Covenant and the cited article above regarding universality with these three crucial statements by Abdul-Baha published prior to his death in the *Star of the West* November 23, 1920, p 243:

> "In New York City, July, 1912, Abdul-Baha said to several believers: 'Any one quoting me must have authority written either with my own hand, or Tablets signed with my seal. Otherwise these statements do not belong to me. Every instruction, every teaching that I desire to spread I will write with my own hand. You must know this generally. Never accept any statement without my writing which is signed and sealed—any statement."

"In Egypt, in August, 1913, Abdul-Baha stated (Mirza Ahmad Sohrab interpreting): 'When in America I repeatedly said that no one must believe one word said by another regarding any commands, teachings or statements made by me unless they can produce the same in writing over my signature."

"That which has come forth from the Center of the Covenant you must take fast hold of. That which issues from my lips and that which is written with my pen is the Reality. With this you can irrigate the vineyard of God. With this you can make the tree of the Cause of God become verdant. Through this Name the Kingdom of God will be spread all over the world. Through this the Sun of Reality will shine. Through this the clouds of Mercy will pour down. Whosoever utters a word you must ask: 'Where is the authority of the Center of the Covenant? Show it.' Without this you must not listen to him. If an angel comes down from heaven and has no authority from the Center of the Covenant, you must require his authority. Otherwise the vineyard will become withered and dry. This is the reality."

About the Reform Bahai Faith

The Reform Bahai Faith affirms the universal spiritual and moral principles taught in all of the great religious traditions. Similar to Mahayana Buddhism and the Buddha's Example of compassion, Reform Bahais believe the Example set by Abdul-Baha during his travels to Europe and the United States in the early 20th century, an Example of universal love and brotherhood, was perhaps his greatest teaching.

As Abdul-Baha often suggested, far from having the exclusive truth and the fanaticism to which that notion has so often led, Reform Bahais look to what is universal and non-creedal in the world's religious experience, and include prayers and meditations from other religions in their private and community worship, listen to and learn from God's other religions—all of which is to say the Reform Bahai Faith has moved on from its historical and cultural roots, as all living religions have and do, and is now a global, universal faith.

Abdul-Baha taught that the Bahai Movement was a way for people of all religious persuasions to come together in neutral territory and worship the Divine Being in a mutually respectful atmosphere of peace and harmony. Speaking in England, he said, "You can be a Bahai-Christian, a Bahai-Freemason, a Bahai-Jew, a Bahai-Muhammadan."

Reform Bahais believe Abdul-Baha's Interpretation for the modern world of his Father Baha'u'llah's Teachings is much more profound than the prevailing conception of religion.

Speaking in Europe and North America from 1911 to 1913, Abdul-Baha stated on a number of occasions that he was a man just like anyone else and that the Bahai Faith could not be organized, yet often spoke paradoxically of the growth of the Bahai community throughout the world, grounded in democratic pluralism. Known during Abdul-Baha's time as the Bahai Movement or Cause, the Reform Bahai Faith is not an organization, but a way of life.

More "Protestant" along the lines, in some ways, of Unitarian Universalism or other similarly liberal denominations, Reform Bahais believe it's largely the responsibility of the individual to read the Bahai Writings and prayerfully decide, prayerfully discern, how to follow the spiritual message of Baha'u'llah, Founder of the Bahai Faith, and those of Abdul-Baha, the Interpreter of Baha'u'llah's Covenant, striving for spiritual development and service to humankind.

God has created the individual soul to develop in the integrity and freedom of his or her own search for spiritual maturity and conscience, through prayer and meditation, transforming the community and the world one soul at a time, achieving the timeless goal of self-sacrificing love, compassion, and service to humanity.

In practice, there are individual Reform Bahais who follow all or many commonly shared Bahai forms and teachings observed by other Baha'i denominations because they themselves believe they should or want to; not because they're pressured into them. There are other Reform Bahais who don't feel comfortable with one thing or another, believing perhaps the time is not right for themselves and others, or the particular teaching may be more culturally bound to the past than the more universal principles of Baha'u'llah. Reform Bahais follow Abdul-Baha's 1912 Authentic Covenant, which he delivered publicly in New York City, a broad, open, loving vision of God's relation to humanity.

While emphasizing what is universal in humanity's religious experience, Baha'u'llah taught the changing, evolutionary, and progressive nature of religious truth, demonstrating it by his own example and teaching which evolved away from much of the teaching of his forerunner the Bab. Similarly, Abdul-Baha demonstrated essentially a re-Interpretation of Baha'u'llah's teachings for the modern world. Reform Bahais do not regard the Bahai message as a rigid set of unchanging and inflexible doctrines and formulas. Nor is the universality of the Bahai vision frozen in a form subordinate to the exclusivism of the

Judeo-Christian or Islamic and Sufi cultural heritage of the Bahai Faith. The universal, global Teachings of Baha'u'llah transcend the limitations of all past Dispensations, inspire and envision a new spiritual worldview and civilization.

Baha'u'llah and Abdul-Baha taught that it is the Spirit that is important, not form, doctrine, or organization. Accordingly, God is interested in the human heart, sincere worship, communion, and prayer, the individual cultivating the virtues of the spirit in selfless service to humanity, in practice and deed, not merely doctrine and theory, in every walk of life, respecting the unique cultures of the earth, even while revering what's universal or held in common by humankind.

Abdul-Baha envisioned the Bahai House of Worship as open to the faithful of all religions and traditions, as a place of universal prayer and meditation, not exclusively Bahai. Consequently, Reform Bahais honor the spirit wherever it is found and expressed in the writings and oral traditions of wisdom and belief.

Following Abdul-Baha, Reform Bahais elect Spiritual Assemblies, with nine members, for community consultation and guidance. Largely "congregational" in structure, local communities are independent grass-root associations, though they will ultimately elect national and an international unit with non-binding advisory and coordinating duties and responsibilities. While Abdul-Baha stated he had not "appointed" anyone to succeed him, he did not mean that the local, democratically elected assembly could not appoint people to serve in any position necessary, "to engage in service of the Kingdom." At every level of Bahai consultation, the independence and integrity of the individual is preserved.

Reform Bahais believe Baha'u'llah taught that the separation of church and state is the Will of God and distance themselves from any interpretation of an eventual Bahai theocracy, following Abdul-Baha's vision of a global spiritual democracy, enriched by pluralism. At the deepest level Bahai universality understands its own claim to spiritual truth to critique itself and open to and merge with every breath from heaven.

Reform Bahais are free to express, write, and publish, without any type of "review" or censorship. The Reform Bahai Faith does not teach or practice shunning, nor any form of excommunication, following Abdul-Baha's teaching that "The conscience of man is sacred and to be respected."

February 2010

Respecting the Conscience of Man

June 27, 2000

Juan R. I. Cole. *Modernity and Millennium: The Genesis of the Baha'i Faith in the Nineteenth-Century Middle East.* Columbia University Press, 1997.

In his conclusion, which would never have passed the system of censorship, "Baha'i review," which the UHJ imposes on all publications brought out under its tight control, Professor Cole, of the Department of History at the University of Michigan, quite accurately identifies the distortions that have been wreaked upon Baha'u'llah's Teachings:

> Some contemporary leaders of the Baha'i Faith have given answers increasingly similar to those of fundamentalists, stressing scriptural literalism, patriarchy, theocracy, censorship, intellectual intolerance, and denying key democratic values. While the values of the nineteenth-century Baha'i movement, which was far more tolerant, continue to exist as a minority view, by the late 1990s a different set of emphases prevailed (196).

Cole himself and many others have suffered at the hands of the fundamentalists who have taken control of the religion:

> The rise of academic Baha'i scholarship has caused tension in the community, whose present-day leadership tends to be fundamentalist and antiliberal in orientation, and this has led to pressure on a number of prominent academics to resign or dissociate themselves from the movement (201).

These same forces of fundamentalist orthodoxy are evident on talk.religion.bahai and alt.religion.bahai on Usenet for impartial viewers to witness. They will be evident to all perceptive observers of whatever forum Bahais may be trying to control and influence. Both my and Cole's websites provide essential documentation along these lines. It should be noted that the Universal House of Justice has actively worked through the BCCA (Bahai Computer and Communications Association) to suppress all links to websites with other than its own "comprehensive" point of view on such major portals as Yahoo.com, Excite.com, and other search engines. The UHJ has gone even further by advising Bahais to remove any link whatsoever to Professor Cole's website.

As a Bahai since 1976, I myself have always found especially repulsive the manner in which Bahai fundamentalists attempt to manipulate the institutions and leaders of government, the United Nations, and public opinion, while pretending to values they deride in private or at Bahai-only meetings.

Ultimately, it is the Bahai Universal House of Justice that is responsible for the perversion and corruption of such clear and elevating teachings of Baha'u'llah and Abdul-Baha as the following:

> These are effectual and sufficient proofs that the conscience of man is sacred and to be respected; and that liberty thereof produces widening of ideas, amendment of morals, improvement of conduct, disclosure of the secrets of the contingent world. Abdul-Baha, *A Traveler's Narrative* (91).

The UHJ is also in the end responsible for inciting Bahai fanatics and fundamentalists to attack other Bahais and non-Bahais merely for their views expressed on and off line in free forums of public discussion.

Professor Cole's *Modernity and the Millennium* will remain, for many years to come, the most important book available on the Baha'i Faith. His discussion of its historical development within the intellectual milieu of progressive 19th Century thought is particularly brilliant and insightful.

The American Bahai Mixture

July 25, 2006

William Garlington. *The Baha'i Faith in America*. Praeger. 2005.

After becoming a Baha'i in the 1960s, William Garlington moved to Australia, where he wrote his dissertation on Baha'i mass teaching in Malwa, India, eventually returning to the United States. For over twenty-five years, he taught religious studies in Australia and the US. In the 1980s he withdrew his membership in the Baha'i Faith, essentially he says over doctrinal issues relating to revelation and the infallibility of Baha'i institutions.

Since the majority of available books on the Baha'i Faith are written by members and must be officially "reviewed" and approved by Baha'i institutions, Garlington's book is important as a rare attempt at an objective appraisal of the Baha'i Faith and its actual history and practice. Life as it is lived, versus theory. The last few decades have been crucial years for revealing much that has hitherto been largely kept hidden from public knowledge. Garlington's experience as both a believer and a scholar of religion serves him well in his often insightful treatment of the major conflicts and disagreements over theological issues.

More than any other book to date, Garlington reveals the extent to which people have been harassed and hounded out of the Baha'i Faith for the slightest deviation of thought and belief, even to the extent of having to spurn their own family, with the roots of such treatment extending back into the earliest years of Bahai history in the United States. While he discusses or mentions the incidents surrounding Ruth White, Mirza Ahmad Sohrab, Julie Chanler, and Mason Remey, among others, I do believe he fails adequately to investigate the circumstances of their individual beliefs and basically repeats the usual official line that dismisses all of them as heretics or "covenant breakers." For instance, Lewis Stuyvesant Chanler was the Lieutenant Governor of the State of New York in 1906 and the Democratic candidate for Governor in 1908, facts always conveniently left out of "reviewed" Baha'i publications. Neither he nor his wife were fringe elements as they are so often portrayed. Both were from prestigious families. Ruth White has routinely been misrepresented as the later devotee of an Indian guru, as though nothing more need be said, playing on both Islamic and Western prejudices, which nevertheless entirely evades answering her charge that the leading British Museum handwriting expert of the day, Dr. Charles Ainsworth Mitchell, judged Abdul-Baha's will and testament a fraud. Garlington brings no new material, archival or documentary, to the understanding of such incidents of excommunication (takfir). Sohrab's own book *Broken Silence* raises many profound issues that neither Garlington nor any other researcher has made sufficient effort to address or understand. Other scholars might very well want to start by independently examining what actually happened in such cases.

Of even more interest to me is Garlington's discussion of the many incidents that have developed in connection with the rise of the Internet during the mid and late '90s since I participated in the long battle to create what is still the only uncensored forum for the discussion of the Baha'i Faith, talk.religion.bahai on Usenet. As with China, the Baha'i Faith found itself confronted for the first time with a means of communication it couldn't entirely control and silence. Like China, the Baha'i Faith has developed an apologetical cadre for monitoring, influencing and controlling discussion on the Internet. Yet the early atmosphere of the talisman mailing list, as with other online forums, was euphoric with new found liberty and freedom for Baha'is to speak honestly about the Baha'i Faith, setting off paroxysms of outrage and self-righteous allegations by fundamentalists that others were "tending toward covenant breaking," "divisive," "not Baha'i," and so on. Much of it, along with other incidents touching on religious freedom, can still be found documented on the Internet through University of Michigan Professor Juan Cole's website, my own, www.fglaysher.com/bahaicensorship, and the Google Groups archive for talk.religion.bahai (or Archive.org).

Another shortcoming in Garlington's book is that while his Conclusion acknowledges that "vocal and liberal Baha'is" are becoming "an ever-decreasing minority," he fails to examine sufficiently why that is, namely, the extreme and alarming tactics used to drive liberals out of the Baha'i Faith, exemplified in the attacks on Ruth White and Ahmad Sohrab—the most vicious shunning and slandering techniques used by perhaps any religion in America today. Official Baha'i sources and the Internet abound with examples. Garlington barely scratches the surface of the extent to which "hikmat," so-called wisdom, operates in Baha'i history, as do "taqlid," blind obedience, and "takfir," excommunication. Much more needs to be said in this regard.

The real test of any religious ethic is not the treatment of those who keep their mouths closed, never thinking or questioning anything (taqlid), but rather the treatment of those writers and scholars of capacity, deeply grounded in the intellectual history and traditions of their culture. The Baha'i Faith has so thoroughly failed that test, especially during the last few decades, that no individual or country should take its claims at face value without reading and reflecting on such books as William Garlington's. It should be noted that the December 2005 *Library Journal* review of Garlington's book, by William P. Collins, a conservative apologist for Baha'i orthodoxy, employs the usual Baha'i tactic of discrediting and slandering any dissident opinion, while recommending books that have passed "Baha'i review," in reality, censorship. The reader might want to reflect on the fact that William P. Collins is a librarian at the Library of Congress, yet readily uses his position to defend a system of administration regularly attacking the liberal values that make a library worthy of the name possible and to discourage acquisition librarians from ordering Garlington's book.

In his closing paragraph Garlington urges the Baha'i leadership to manifest a higher degree of wisdom, echoing all too much for me the practices of "hikmat" that resulted, in the Western world, often in the most cynical manipulation of the "rank and file." Rather, I would say, what's required is a higher level of normal decency, humility, and respect for the individual's freedom and liberty of conscience, along the lines of Isaiah Berlin. It doesn't take much wisdom to realize what kind of world the present arrogant and utopian administration would create. One needs only to look at American Baha'i history and the abuse of now countless individuals and families.

In addition to Garlington's book, the serious student of Bahai history should also read Professor Juan Cole's *Modernity and the Millennium*, and Peter Smith's *Babi and Bahai Religions*. The few Christian polemical writers, who have bothered to write anything, can't hold a match to those who have been burned by the shunning and slander of Baha'i fundamentalism. Yet these authors merely touch the surface of too many incidents that raise serious questions for any American concerned about preserving religious freedom and liberty. There is a very real need for fresh research and excavation of any surviving original material that might throw more light on the major conflicts of American Bahai history. While Garlington seldom moves very far beyond the received version of American Baha'i history, his book is at least the first written by a scholar trying to discover essentially what Edward Gibbon called the "inevitable mixture of error and corruption" that a religion contracts "in a long residence upon earth," versus the predictably self-serving propaganda of the converted. The publisher Praeger is to be applauded for its commitment to free speech and discussion.

Bahai Church and State

December 15, 2007

Church and State: A Postmodern Political Theology. Sen McGlinn. Leiden, 2005.

In light of the Haifan Universal House of Justice having declared Sen McGlinn a "*kafir*," infidel, shortly after the 2005 publication of *Church and State*, the book resonates with many unintended ironies and contradictions. Written in hope of "recasting," "reformulating," "reinterpreting," "refocusing," and "rethinking" the contemporary Baha'i understanding of Baha'u'llah's Teachings, Sen McGlinn has been thrown into the role of heretical Bahai theologian, denounced and excommunicated, tossed out of the church he had hoped to save from its own gross ignorance, anti-intellectualism, and fanaticism.

It will be interesting to see if McGlinn learns from the experience or is crushed by it. No greater test can be given an intelligent soul. It either calls out of one's being an even deeper engagement with evil and truth, a struggle for clarity and understanding, or it destroys the fragile foundations of the self, exposing the shallowness of the structure one has built on. Nothing could prove his thesis more than the reactionary attack of the corrupt, decadent, and fraudulent universal house of justice.

Setting aside what he himself realizes is a tedious academic literature review of Islamic and Bahai sources on the relations of church and state and blind belief in theocracy, giving the benighted sources way too much attention, McGlinn presents, as a Bahai theologian, not a historian or apologist, the first glimmer of a deeply considered vision of Baha'u'llah's Faith in the post-modern world. Far from a simplistic fanatical rejection of Enlightenment values, McGlinn defends their worth and realizes that, on the deepest spiritual level, so did

Baha'u'llah—He Himself teaches that the separation of church and state is the way things should be, is God's Will, and not something to be overturned and supplanted with a despicable theocracy of one sort or another—Christian, Islamic, Baha'i, or whatever. Worldly power and coercion should be in the hands of those pragmatists who live with two feet on the ground and are not tempted by religious visions of spiritual utopias and New Jerusalems descending upon the earth at any cost. No wonder the organization based upon a spurious will and testament has pronounced his ideas and book "*takfir*," anathema. He has gone deeper into Baha'u'llah's Teachings than they can ever hope to achieve.

In a key passage of the book, McGlinn writes,

> What is needed is not simply to recast Bahai thought in contemporary terms, or to hold the theological thinking of the Bahais up for critical examination in the light of Bahai scripture . . . but rather to drag Bahai thinking bodily from one world-view into the next. We can scarcely understand, now, the extent to which the Christians of the second and third centuries saw their religion in terms set by the shape of Roman society and the Roman state. If we do focus on that, we also see the magnitude of the transition initiated by Augustine's theology, in disentangling the Christian religion from outdated suppositions about society (10).

The historical sweep of McGlinn's vision is truly awe-inspiring. He alludes elsewhere to Plato and Ibn Farabi. I wish he would have discussed Ibn Khaldun, instead of merely relegating him to the bibliography, since he understood so profoundly the extent to which Islam had departed from its early beginnings and had been transformed into a separation of the practical control of the state under royal princes. Ibn Khaldun is the *locus classicus* of that realization about Islam. Analogously, McGlinn sets his entire discussion in a context and at a level that addresses the postmodern dilemmas that confront world civilization in our age and articulates a persuasive argument that Baha'u'llah can only be properly understood from such a vantage point, as a prophet of post-modernity, laying the foundation and rationale for a new stage of human evolution and civilization, material, political, and spiritual. Elsewhere, in his article "Baha'i Meets Globalisation," McGlinn states it quite directly, "Baha'u'llah must be re-envisioned as the prophet of post-modernity" (14).

McGlinn's discussion of Postmodernism is unsatisfyingly brief, perhaps a reflection of the paucity of his own knowledge and omnipresent Bahai Philistinism, but, in a sketchy way, demonstrates his understanding of the issues involved, including the literary and philosophical dimensions of the underlying spiritual and religious disruptions and upheavals, which he barely touches upon. Reading a book written by a Bahai scholar, one can't expect much when it comes to culture. They are usually specialists in one dimension or another of Islam, which helps them in some ways but blinds them in others. Like many Westerners and Bahais, they are often lacking in knowledge of their own culture, especially its philosophical, political, and aesthetic underpinnings, or have imbibed the anti-Western mentality and Philistinism of Islamic sources when it comes to the arts, typified in the treatment of Salman Rushdie. I am accustomed to, and prefer, Postmodernism in literary terms, its most consciously articulate and allusive form.

Part of his discussion draws from sociological studies of globalization and technology, which emphasize the "functional differentiation" and "individualization" of modern life, the compartmentalization of experience, producing, in Enlightenment terms, pluralism and relativism, all of which gives a much needed fresh, intelligent context for discussions of the Bahai Teachings, and a vastly more compelling framework within which to understand "*the world we live in*," of "lasting pluralism," contrasted with the current unthinking fundamentalism of the current Haifan denomination, for whom Baha'u'llah's writings have become a static, literal, unchanging fossil that they seek to cram into the "now empty socket where 'religion' belongs," the socket of their antiquated conception of a new world order, merely imitating past dispensations, imagining their assumed "infallibility" enables them to know better than Baha'u'llah.

Nothing could prove how wrong such benighted doctrinaire fanaticism is than its treatment of such an intelligent, outstanding mind as Sen McGlinn. One only need recall the similar witch hunts and expulsions of Juan Cole of the University of Michigan, Linda and John Walbridge of Indiana University, Denis MacEoin of England, and other gifted scholars and writers. The corruption runs, though, much deeper than McGlinn even realizes. There's a naivete to many of his comments. His courting a particularly bigoted and fanatical Baha'i pseudo-scholar, a few times in the book, cannot appear as anything but ridiculously misconceived, all the more so given her subsequent hatchet job on his work, the only thing she's capable of writing.

From such a perspective, *Church and State* presents a sad spectacle. He clearly is trying to reform and renew the intellectual and spiritual stagnation the Baha'i Faith has fallen into, but it is while courting Torquemada, without having the courage to confront the inquisitor. Torquemada demonstrates no such scruples about Sen McGlinn. Many souls died on the rack. Few, like Martin Luther, understood that the unmitigated corruption revealed a disease so evil as to require a more profound engagement with the issues involved, a return to, and renewal of, its deepest principles, to truly "re-invent itself." McGlinn has rightly understood those principles, as Baha'u'llah did, "in terms of globalisation, to offer itself as a means of giving meaning to a post-modern society." Similarly, McGlinn realizes the theocratic interpretation is wrong and a complete departure from Baha'u'llah. Whether he will have the strength to allow himself to acknowledge that the root of the problem is the fraudulent will and testament of Abdul-Baha of 1921, and almost everything produced by it, remains to be seen. His many quotations of Shoghi Effendi may indicate he'll never be able to regain an independent Bahai perspective that would allow him to search out the truth for himself and to return to the actual writings and teachings of Abdul-Baha and his 1912 Covenant, as well as acknowledge Abdul-Baha repeatedly taught, in a sense difficult to understand, that "The Bahai Movement is not an organization."

Souls can be crushed by suffering, by coming up against challenges to their inmost beliefs and sense of being, of identity. Some cravenly kiss the hand that whipped them, the dream of every tyrant. Many, if not most, go down or walk away from such ultimate confrontations and struggles for understanding and belief. Whatever the outcome for McGlinn's own personal spiritual battles, and whether he breaks through to new and deeper insights, he has broken new ground for Bahais who have already learned from their experiences and have truly moved on to Reform and renew Baha'u'llah's Faith in the globalized world of post-modernity.

I agree with McGlinn's evaluation of the ecumenical role of the Mashriqu'l-Adkar or Bahai House of Worship, in this book and his articles. Baha'u'llah and Abdul-Baha teach that it should be open to all people for prayer and worship, not merely Bahais, and the social, educational, medical, and economic dependencies and charities related to it are crucial to both community growth and the transformation of global society. McGlinn explains, quoting Abdul-Baha:

> Religious and cultural pluralism is here to stay and will increase, because of mobility, individual choice, and the fact that successful modern states cannot have a religious policy. The project of the Mashriqu'l-Adhkar is to create an ecumenical devotional sphere, not bound to a particular doctrinal system, and open to a variety of popular devotion: "In brief, the purpose of places of worship . . . is simply that of unity . . . that is why His Holiness Baha'u'llah has commanded that a place be built

> for all the religionists of the world; that all religions and races and sects may gather together; that the Oneness of the human world may be proclaimed."
>
> . . . In the modern world, the progression from a sectarian role to a religion informing society and providing religious services to all society—a 'church' in the Weberian sense—can be achieved not by winning state patronage but by developing devotional, aesthetic and intellectual forms that sustain and are sustained by the diversity of popular religious feeling in a pluralist society (143).

Much has been damaged and lost by setting aside Abdul-Baha's unifying vision for the theocratic temptation, relegating people to the paternalism of the derisive "rank and file" and "popular devotion."

God creates both the individual and the community, and neither truly exists without the other, especially in a globalized society:

> Globalisation is a dynamic package in which individualisation is the underlying drive, and functional differentiation (including the separation of church and state), feminisation, global integration, pluralism and relativism are the results. This is in effect a new world, entailing a new principle of individual identity, and the transition places great demands on individuals' capacity to adapt (144).

The House of Worship is more than a Bahai mosque or church. A whole new conception of sacred, religious space is required to understand it. After God, the individual stands at its center, independently seeking truth, in unity with humanity, not merely other "believers."

McGlinn rightly argues it is the role of religion, in Baha'u'llah's postmodern conception of the relation of church and state, that carries the responsibility for inculcating morality and virtue into the individual and community. The problem of how to instill altruism to resist extremely self-serving individualism and license stems from the very beginning of the Enlightenment and modernity, with the separation of the state from the church in the late 1700s, with the *philosophes,* Voltaire, Rousseau, and other writers. The best social thinkers of our own time have struggled with the reverberations of that problem, Robert Bellah, Christopher Lasch, and Gertrude Himmelfarb, to name a few. Baha'u'llah preserves that separation as the Will of God, making it a religious duty to support and participate in a just government, delegating the cultivation of virtue into the "hearts of men" to his followers and to all religions. Religion and state complement one another in an unprecedented balance in human religious history, instead of a destructive contest convulsing society, though religion retains the duty to critique government, in service to God, virtue, and humanity. It is not enough for a religion to say all this; it must prove it. The currently dominant interpretation of the Bahai Faith hasn't done too well in that regard. Mirza Ahmad Sohrab realized in his courageous book *Broken Silence* that the Baha'i organization under Shoghi Effendi had become corrupt and destructive of the spiritual life and independence of the individual, seeking to strip the soul of the freedom of conscience and the gift of the will with which God has endowed human beings. Shades of Dostoyevsky.

McGlinn's *Church and State* might have benefitted from his pondering this passage from Ibn Khaldun's *An Introduction to History,* of 1377, echoing, I would say, Plato's *Republic*:

> All this has its origin in group feeling.... Luxury wears out royal authority and overthrows it. ...Eventually, a great change takes place in the world, such as the transformation of a religion, or the disappearance of a civilization, or something else willed by the power of

> God. Then, royal authority is transferred from one group to another—to the one God permits to effect that change.

Such a "transformation of a religion" has been long under way for the Bahai Faith, not only postmodern society and Western civilization. The dominant "group-feeling" of the Haifans began to sink into "luxury" with the passing of Abdul-Baha and the imposition of the falsified will and testament of 1921, leading to many mistakes and excesses, not the least of which was the inhuman destruction of families by requiring husbands and wives and children to shun one another over doctrinal absurdities. Many tens of thousands of Bahais realize there is something extremely unloving and wrong about the naked royal emperor; many have been driven out like McGlinn, for possessing a brain and soul; many others are waiting, looking, searching for the Will of God, for the Bahai theologian who can help them understand His Will. Sen McGlinn has earned the honor of possibly being the first Bahai worthy of the role. As has often been observed, intellectual, spiritual, and cultural history is strewn with examples of scholars and writers merely laying a brick or two in the foundation of the next generation. No small achievement in itself, but not the lofty edifice.

McGlinn's intelligent though flawed book should help seeking souls in their quest for a world beyond the postmodern, offering a way to understand Baha'u'llah's "lasting pluralism" in a global world of multiplicity, where religion is the mirror of "individual distinctiveness, not of collective identity."

A Response to Takfir[1]

Published in "Challenging Apostasy: Responses to Moojan Momen's 'Marginality and Apostasy in the Baha'i Community.'" *Religion* 38 No 4 2008, 384-393.

Moojan Momen's paragraph about me in his article 'Marginality and Apostasy in the Baha'i Community,' *Religion* 37 2007, 187–209, under the guise of scholarly content and factual statement, is a litany of falsehoods and distortions about who I am.

Holding two degrees from the University of Michigan, I studied there with the poet Robert Hayden, who was a Baha'i, and edited both Hayden's *Collected Prose* (University of Michigan Press, 1984) and his *Collected Poems* (Liveright, 1985). A man of formidable intellectual integrity, Robert Hayden loathed fundamentalist Baha'is. Sharing his assessment, I discuss Hayden's actual views on the Baha'i Faith at length in my essay about him in my recently published *The Grove of the Eumenides: Essays on Literature, Criticism, and Culture* (2007). I have also published three other books of poetry and prose, have a forthcoming volume in Spring 2008, and have been a Fulbright-Hays scholar to China and an NEH scholar on India; but since I'm supposed to be a 'marginal' Baha'i 'apostate,'

---

[1] The scholar Bernard Lewis defined *takfir* as "recognizing and denouncing apostasy," labeling people "kafir" or infidels, and issuing "fatwas" against them—practices Baha'u'llah and Abdul-Baha specifically rejected, teaching tolerance of different religious views congruent with modern Western custom and practice—indicative of the worst in the Iranian Shiite millennialism of the Baha'i Faith, a Scientology-like criminal cult, based on a fraudulent document, attempting to create a global theocracy by deceiving and brainwashing its unsuspecting members into a false version of its history and using them to carry out Baha'i jihads against dissenters and critics.

Momen, like all zealous Baha'i apologists, can only treat people with caricature and slander, as has been done by Baha'i fundamentalists for over a decade on talk.religion.bahai and elsewhere online.

Implicitly deriding my four years of community college teaching, Momen conveniently leaves out that I taught English literature and rhetoric for seven years at Gunma University (Japan), Illinois State University, and Oakland University.

Momen claims that I had 'personal clashes with Iranian Baha'is' (198). Apparently someone thought so and reported something to someone. What is the accusation and who is my accuser? In Western law, the accused have the right to know and confront the accuser, in order to protect the innocent from libel.

Haifan Baha'is have often denied the existence of other Bahai denominations. Following that pattern, Momen implies that the Reform Bahai Faith does not exist. The Reform Bahai Faith began August 19, 2004, although its roots go back to Ruth White, Mirza Ahmad Sohrab, Julie Chanler, and other early Baha'is who were similarly maligned for not accepting the fundamentalist interpretation of Baha'u'llah's Teachings, based on the purported will and testament of Abdu'l-Baha, written by the family of Shoghi Effendi, and pronounced a fraud in 1930 by Dr. C. Ainsworth Mitchell of the British Museum.

The Reform Bahai Faith is already much larger than any other Bahai denomination, including the three combined that the NSA of Wilmette is currently suing in the US District Court of Northern Illinois.

My website 'The Baha'i Faith & Religious Freedom of Conscience' may be the most comprehensive effort made to document the fanaticism that has taken over the largest Baha'i denomination. Further details on Baha'i takfir at fglaysher.com/bahaicensorship

APPENDIX

Address upon the Covenant by Abdul-Baha

New York City, June 19th, 1912.
Translated by Dr. Ameen U. Fareed.
Parentheses supplied.

Tomorrow I wish to go to Montclair [New Jersey]. Today is the last day in which we gather together with you to say farewell to you. Therefore, I wish to expound for you an important question, and that question concerns The Covenant.

In former cycles no distinct Covenant had been made in writing by the Supreme Pen; no distinct personage had been appointed to be the Standard differentiating falsehood from truth, so that whatsoever he was to say was to stand as truth and that which he repudiated was to be known as falsehood. At most, His Holiness Jesus Christ gave only an intimation, a symbol, and that was but an indication of the solidity of Peter's faith. When he mentioned his faith, His Holiness said, "Thou art Peter"- which means rock-"and upon this rock will I build my church." This was a sanction of Peter's faith; it was not indicative of his (Peter) being the expounder of the Book, but was a confirmation of Peter's faith.

But in this dispensation of the Blessed Beauty, (Baha'u'llah) among its distinctions is that He did not leave people in perplexity. He entered into a covenant and testament with the people. He appointed a Center of the Covenant. He wrote with His own pen and revealed it in the Kitab-el-Akdas, the Book of Laws, the Book of the Covenant, appointing him (Abdul-Baha) the Expounder of the Book. You must ask him Abdul-Baha) regarding the meanings of the texts of the verses. Whatsoever he says is correct. Outside of this, in numerous tablets He (Baha'u'llah) has explicitly recorded it, with clear, sufficient, valid and forceful statements. In the tablet of The Branch He explicitly states, "Whatsoever The Branch says is right, or correct; and every person must obey The Branch with his life, with his heart, with his tongue. Without his will not a word shall anyone utter." This is an explicit text of the Blessed Beauty. So there is no rescue left for anybody. No soul shall, of himself, speak anything. Whatsoever his (Abdul-Baha's) tongue utters, whatsoever his pen records, that is correct; according to the explicit text of Baha'u'llah in the tablet of The Branch.

His Holiness Abraham covenanted with regard to Moses. His Holiness Moses was the Promised One of Abraham, and He, Moses, covenanted with regard to His Holiness Christ, saying that Christ was the Promised One. His Holiness Christ covenanted with regard to His Holiness "The Paraclete," which means His Holiness Mohammed. His Holiness Mohammed covenanted as regards The Bab, whom He called, "My Promised One," His Holiness The Bab, in all His books, in all His epistles, explicitly covenanted with regard to the Blessed Beauty, Baha'u'llah—that Baha'u'llah was the Promised One of His Holiness The Bab. His Holiness Baha'u'llah covenanted, not that I (Abdul-Baha) am the Promised One, but that Abdul-Baha is the Expounder of the Book and The Center of His Covenant, and that the Promised One of Baha'u'llah will appear after one thousand or thousands of years. This is the Covenant which Baha'u'llah made. If a person shall deviate, he is not acceptable at the Threshold of Baha'u'llah. In case of difference—Abdul-Baha must be consulted. They must revolve around his good pleasure. After Abdul-Baha—whenever the Universal House of Justice is organized it will ward off differences.

Now I pray for you that GOD may aid you, may confirm you, may appoint you for His service; that He may suffer you to be as radiant candles; that He may accept you in His Kingdom; that He may make you the cause of the spread of the light of Baha'u'llah in these countries, and that the teachings of Baha'u'llah may be spread broadcast.

I pray for you, and I am pleased with all of you, each one, one by one; and I pray that GOD may aid and confirm you. From Montclair I will come back to you. New York is favored,

I go away and I come back to it. The friends in New York must appreciate this. At present, farewell to you!

Published November the Twelfth,
nineteen hundred and twelve.

The ninety-fifth anniversary of the birth
of Baha'u'llah.

The Bahai Assembly of Washington, D.C.

[Source: From *Bahai Teaching: Quotations from the Bahai Sacred Writings and several articles upon the History and Aims of the Teaching*. Charles Mason Remey. Published in pamphlet form at various times and bound into this booklet in the month of July nineteen hundred and seventeen at Washington in the District of Columbia. Booklet in Michigan State Library. Main, Dew 299. 15R38bt C. 1]

[See the following pages for a facsimile.]

9

ADDRESS UPON THE COVENANT BY ABDUL-BAHA

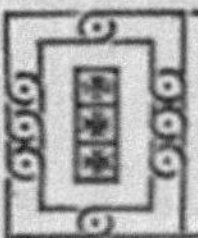

ADDRESS

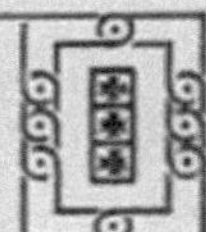

NEW YORK CITY, JUNE 19th, 1912.

Translated by DR. AMEEN U. FAREED.
Parentheses Supplied.

Tomorrow I wish to go to Montclair. Today is the last day in which we gather together with you to say farewell to you. Therefore, I wish to expound for you an important question, and that question concerns The Covenant.

In former cycles no distinct Covenant had been made in writing by the Supreme Pen; no distinct personage had been appointed to be the Standard differentiating falsehood from truth, so that whatsoever he was to say was to stand as truth and that whcih he repudiated was to be known as falsehood. At most, His Holiness Jesus Christ gave only an intimation, a symbol, and that was but an indication of the solidity of Peter's faith. When he mentioned his faith, His Holiness said, "Thou art Peter"—which means rock—"and upon this rock will I build my church". This was a sanction of Peter's faith; it was not indicative of his (Peter) being the expounder of the Book, but was a confirmation of Peter's faith.

But in this dispensation of the Blessed Beauty, (Baha'o'llah) among its distinctions is that He did not leave people in perplexity. He entered into a covenant and testament with the people. He appointed a Center of the Covenant. He wrote with His own pen and revealed it in the Kitab-el-Akdas, the Book of Laws, the Book of the Covenant, appointing him (Abdul-Baha) the Expounder of the Book. You must ask him (Abdul-Baha) regarding the meanings of the texts of the verses. Whatsoever he says is correct. Outside of this, in numerous tablets He (Baha'-o'llah) has explicitly recorded it, with clear, sufficient, valid and forceful statements. In the tablet of The Branch He explicitly states, "Whatsoever The Branch says is right, or correct; and every person must obey The Branch with his life, with his heart, with his tongue. Without his will, not a word shall anyone utter." This is an explicit text of the Blessed Beauty. So there is no rescue left for anybody. No soul shall, of himself, speak anything. Whatsoever his (Abdul-Baha's) tongue utters, whatsoever his pen records, that is correct; according to the explicit text of Baha'o'llah in the tablet of The Branch.

His Holiness Abraham covenanted with regard to Moses. His Holiness Moses was the Promised One of Abraham, and He, Moses, covenanted with regard to His Holiness Christ, saying that Christ was the Promised One. His Holiness Christ covenanted with regard to His Holiness "The Paraclete," which means His Holiness Mohammed. His Holiness Mohammed covenanted as regards The Bab, whom He called, "My Promised One," His Holiness The Bab, in all His books, in all His epistles, explicitly covenanted with regard to the Blessed Beauty, Baha'o'llah—that Baha'o'llah was the Promised One of His Holiness The Bab. His Holiness Baha'o'llah covenanted, not that I (Abdul-Baha) am the Promised One, but that Abdul-Baha is the Expounder of the Book and The Center of His Covenant, and that the Promised One of Baha'o'llah will appear after one thousand or thousands of years. This is the Covenant which Baha'o'llah made. If a person shall deviate, he is not acceptable at the Threshold of Baha'o'llah. In case of difference—Abdul-Baha must be consulted. They must revolve around his good pleasure. After Abdul-Baha—whenever the Universal House of Justice is organized it will ward off differences.

Now I pray for you that GOD may aid you, may confirm you, may appoint you for His service; that He may suffer you to be as radiant candles; that He may accept you in His Kingdom; that He may make you the cause of the spread of the light of Baha'o'llah in these countries, and that the teachings of Baha'o'llah may be spread broadcast.

I pray for you, and I am pleased with all of you, each one, one by one; and I pray that GOD may aid and confirm you. From Montclair I will come back to you. New York is favored, I go away and I come back to it. The friends in New York must appreciate this. At present, farewell to you!

Published November the Twelfth,
nineteen hundred and twelve.

The ninety-fifth anniversary of the birth
of Baha'o'llah.

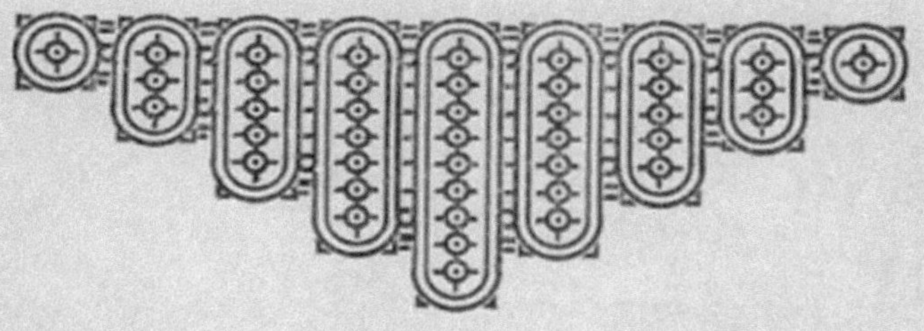

NOTICE

Copies of this pamphlet "The Covenant," may be had at the following rates, which include postage:

1000	Copies	-	-	$20.00
500	"	-	-	11.00
100	"	-	-	2.50
50	"	-	-	1.50
25	"	-	-	1.00

Apply to

The Bahai Assembly of Washington

Wilkins Building,

WASHINGTON, D. C.

www.ingramcontent.com/pod-product-compliance
Lightning Source LLC
Chambersburg PA
CBHW020548310726
48979CB00008B/1139/J
9780967042114